"The author of Hebrews tells us that we should 'not neglect those in prison.' My experience with the students of the OBU PDP program, including those who have authored chapters in this book, has brought this command to life. These men readily acknowledge their need for Jesus, are on fire to share Jesus with those who don't know him, and are passionate about learning the truths of God's word and passing those truths on to others. The testimonies in this book can help bring this same experience to life for readers and perhaps prompt the same kind of work in other areas of the country and beyond."
—MATTHEW Y. EMERSON, Co-Provost,
Oklahoma Baptist University

"In a place that many consider hopeless, individuals are spreading hope to their incarcerated brothers. The work of Dr. Perkins and Oklahoma Baptist University is changing paradigms behind prison walls and paying dividends for generations of Oklahomans. These stories, written by those going through the OBU Divinity Program, are powerful reminders that no one is too far away from the love of Christ."
—KEVIN J. STITT, Governor, Oklahoma

"From the first narrative story to the last, *Inside Out*—penned by the first cohort class of the Oklahoma Baptist University Prison Divinity Program in the Oklahoma Department of Corrections—affirms and adds further confirmation that the Prison Seminaries Foundation model for inmate theological education does indeed produce 'moral rehabilitation.' The stories of the students are both gripping and inspiring in revealing that a liberal arts education that is bible based and Christ centered can produce culture change even among those incarcerated. I am grateful for the work of Dr. Bruce Perkins, Director, and the support of President Heath Thomas of OBU in making this program a high priority in the legacy of the university. May God continue to bless their work in the years ahead."
—J. DENNY AUTREY, Director of Operations,
Prison Seminaries Foundation

Inside Out

Inside Out

*Transformative Learning Stories
and Strategies from Incarcerated Students*

EDITED BY
BRUCE A. PERKINS
JEANETTA D. SIMS

EPILOGUE BY
Antonio Chiareli

CASCADE Books • Eugene, Oregon

INSIDE OUT
Transformative Learning Stories and Strategies from Incarcerated Students

Copyright © 2026 Wipf and Stock Publishers. All rights reserved. Except for brief quotations in critical publications or reviews, no part of this book may be reproduced in any manner without prior written permission from the publisher. Write: Permissions, Wipf and Stock Publishers, 199 W. 8th Ave., Suite 3, Eugene, OR 97401.

Cascade Books
An Imprint of Wipf and Stock Publishers
199 W. 8th Ave., Suite 3
Eugene, OR 97401

www.wipfandstock.com

PAPERBACK ISBN: 979-8-3852-3129-4
HARDCOVER ISBN: 979-8-3852-3130-0
EBOOK ISBN: 979-8-3852-3131-7

Cataloguing-in-Publication data:

Names: Perkins, Bruce A., editor. | Sims, Jeanetta D., editor.

Title: Inside out : transformative learning stories and strategies from incarcerated students / Bruce A. Perkins and Jeanetta D. Sims, editors.

Description: Eugene, OR: Cascade Books, 2026 | Includes bibliographical references.

Identifiers: ISBN 979-8-3852-3129-4 (paperback) | ISBN 979-8-3852-3130-0 (hardcover) | ISBN 979-8-3852-3131-7 (ebook)

Subjects: LCSH: Prisoners—Education—Oklahoma—United States. | Criminals—Rehabilitation—Oklahoma—United States. | Religious work with prisoners.

Classification: HV8881.3.U5 I37 2026 (paperback) | HV8881 (ebook)

01/23/26

Contents

List of Contributors	ix
Acknowledgments	xi
Abbreviations	xiii
Introduction	xv

PART I. STORIES OF PERSONAL GROWTH LEADING TO COMMUNITY IMPACT

A Sheep Dog's Journey *Joshua Benton*	3
God's Secret Place *Tracey Brown*	11
Bridges *Eric Coager*	20
Worldview and Consistency *Dean Luebberst*	29
Set Up to Be Used *Joe Sanders II*	35
Trash or Treasure? A Discourse on the Value of Christian Liberal Arts Education Among the Incarcerated Population *Aaron Weiland*	47

Field Ministers: Equipped to Serve and Prepared to Return   57
Arturo Welch

PART II. STORIES OF PERSONAL FAILURE LEADING TO TRANSFORMATIONAL ACHIEVEMENT

He Has Always Been There: Education Is a Blessing from God   69
Miguel Caballero

A Mountain I Must Climb   78
Leslie Shayne Smith

A College Education like a Multifunctional Tool   85
Vincent Todd Ochoa

PART III. STORIES OF PERSONAL PERSPECTIVES LEADING TO EMBRACING LEARNING

Finding Purpose While Contributing to the Solution:
Stages of Growth   97
Brett Johnson

For Lack of Knowledge   105
Jordan Miller

Not Perfect Yet Useable   113
Roscoe LaRett Morris

From Death to Life   121
Christopher Whinery

The Christian Liberal Arts: Educating All on the Momentum Inherent in Christian Redemption, Rehabilitation, and Restoration   129
James Joseph Wymer Jr.

You Can, You Will   139
Christopher Evans

CONTENTS

Encouraging Non-Catholics and Non-Protestants
   in Christian Colleges   147
   Edsel Hill

Epilogue   155
   Antonio Chiareli

List of Contributors

JOSHUA BENTON, student of the Prison Divinity Program at Oklahoma Baptist University. He previously served a tour in Iraq with the United States Air Force Reserve.

TRACEY BROWN, student of the Prison Divinity Program at Oklahoma Baptist University.

MIGUEL CABALLERO, student of the Prison Divinity Program at Oklahoma Baptist University.

ANTONIO CHIARELI, Professor of Sociology and Intercultural Studies at Oklahoma Baptist University.

ERIC COAGER, student of the Prison Divinity Program at Oklahoma Baptist University. He is currently a musician and worship leader for the North Church Praise and Worship Team in Lexington, Oklahoma.

CHRISTOPHER EVANS, student of the Prison Divinity Program at Oklahoma Baptist University.

EDSEL HILL, student of the Prison Divinity Program at Oklahoma Baptist University.

BRETT JOHNSON, student of the Prison Divinity Program at Oklahoma Baptist University.

List of Contributors

Dean Luebberst, student of the Prison Divinity Program at Oklahoma Baptist University. He previously served a tour in Afghanistan with the United States Air Force.

Jordan Miller, student of the Prison Divinity Program at Oklahoma Baptist University.

Roscoe Morris, student of the Prison Divinity Program at Oklahoma Baptist University.

Vincent Ochoa, student of the Prison Divinity Program at Oklahoma Baptist University. He is ordained through Friendship Baptist Church of Lawton, Oklahoma.

Bruce A. Perkins, Assistant Professor of Christian Education in the Herschel H. Hobbs School of Theology and Ministry and Director of the Prison Divinity Program at Oklahoma Baptist University.

Joe Sanders II, student of the Prison Divinity Program at Oklahoma Baptist University. He also holds an associate degree in Pastoral Ministries from the International Christian College and Seminary. He is currently a music minister at the Divine Wisdom Worship Center of Lexington, Oklahoma.

Jeanetta D. Sims, Professor in the Marketing Department of the College of Business and former Dean of the Jackson College of Graduate Studies at the University of Central Oklahoma.

Leslie Shayne Smith, student of the Prison Divinity Program at Oklahoma Baptist University.

Aaron Weiland, student of the Prison Divinity Program at Oklahoma Baptist University.

Arturo Welch, student of the Prison Divinity Program at Oklahoma Baptist University.

Christopher Whinery, student of the Prison Divinity Program at Oklahoma Baptist University. He previously served with the United States Air Force.

James Joseph Wymer Jr., student of the Prison Divinity Program at Oklahoma Baptist University. He also holds an associate degree in Behavioral Science through Western Oklahoma State College.

Acknowledgments

WE ARE ESPECIALLY GRATEFUL to the Oklahoma Department of Corrections and Oklahoma Baptist University Prison Divinity Program faculty. Your continued support, belief in this Prison Education program, and commitment to Christian liberal arts education has made it possible to foster an impactful legacy of spiritual development for students and faculty alike.

We are sincerely grateful for the steadfast editorial abilities of Zoe Wright, who has been a phenomenal and persistent partner in bringing this project to fruition. Thank you as well to our publishing team at Cascade Books, for your confidence and commitment to this project. Our vision for this book has been enhanced because of your collective editorial work.

Many thanks as well to our student authors who bravely and transparently shared their spiritual journeys while granting us a view of their lived experiences in Christian liberal arts higher education. Without your courage and contributions, this book project would not be possible.

We wish to thank our group of peer reviewers: John Powell, Tawa Anderson, David Gambo, Matthew Emerson, David Houghton, Edward English, Jessica Rohr, Canaan Crane, Brent Newsom, Micah Meek, Larinee Dennis, Rich Rudebock, Karen Longest, and Brian Camp. Your valuable and timely feedback enabled this project to remain on schedule and yield insights for improved contributor manuscripts.

ACKNOWLEDGMENTS

Finally, our gratitude goes to Oklahoma Baptist University, OBU President Dr. Heath Thomas, and Chaplain Ron Lindsey for cultivating an environment capable of fostering a focus on spiritual formation and transformative learning. May soul work in higher education continue to be nudged and nurtured in future Prison Education programs and projects like this one.

Abbreviations

DOC	Department of Corrections
OBU	Oklahoma Baptist University
ODOC	Oklahoma Department of Corrections
PDP	(The) Prison Divinity Program

Introduction

WEDNESDAY, JANUARY 15, 2020, 2:00 PM. I walked into the Office of the President of Oklahoma Baptist University. I served on his Executive Cabinet, and we frequently visited, so I was accustomed to such meetings. Little did I know this particular conversation would open a dynamic new chapter in my life's story. Dr. Heath Thomas shared with me his vision of taking the mission of the university into the prisons of Oklahoma. He wanted me to take the lead and turn this vision into reality. He wanted to change my task and title to become the inaugural director of this new initiative. Some early conversations with the Oklahoma Department of Corrections had taken place, but there was no written agreement. There were ideas about which prison would host such a program, but no definite location had been determined. There was a degree plan, but it needed to be modified. There were no students. There was no faculty. There were no support staff in place. Oh, and there was no money!

My mind drifted back to forty years earlier when I preached prison revivals in Texas as a twenty-something-year-old pastor. "Lord, were you preparing me for this task forty years ago?" I had found those meetings very fulfilling and witnessed countless men come to faith in Christ, but I had never considered ministering in prison or educating incarcerated students as a vocational choice. Yet, on this day, at this time, it seemed as if everything else I had done through thirty-seven years of ministry had prepared me for launching, directing, and teaching in the Oklahoma Baptist University Prison Divinity Program.

I eagerly accepted Dr. Thomas's assignment. Our first students arrived at our host prison in the spring of 2021. The second began their academic studies in the fall of 2023. All are pursuing a bachelor of arts degree in Christian studies. It is a four-year, 120-credit-hour degree built on a liberal arts foundation. The curriculum and instructors seek to integrate faith with each academic discipline, believing all truth is God's truth. Each class is taught face-to-face at the prison. The program presents the same rigor and high expectations we have for all our students, regardless of which campus they attend. Likewise, each professor is chosen and selected by the same criterion as those who teach on the main campus. The experience of our incarcerated students is as close to that of those on our main campus as we can make it—from classroom paint and décor to learning university traditions and wearing university caps and beanies.

Some may wonder, "Why offer a bachelor's degree to incarcerated individuals, especially those who are serving life sentences without the possibility of parole?" Yet, this is our mission.

> The Prison Divinity Program transforms the lives of incarcerated individuals to redeem both the self and the system through the resurrection power of Jesus Christ by providing a learning environment and program of study that leads to a reformed perspective on life which results in a redirected purpose for life.

Studies have demonstrated both the individual and societal benefits of higher education programs for incarcerated individuals.[1] Most studies link these benefits to a reduction in recidivism. This is logical. Postsecondary education increases one's employability,

---

1. A 2013 study by Rand Corporation (Davis et al., "Evaluating the Effectiveness") found that formerly incarcerated individuals who received education while in prison return to prison at a dramatically lower rate than those who did not engage in postsecondary education. Data supplied by Emory University indicates the recidivism rate falls increasingly lower as higher levels of education are attained (see Christian, "We Can't Afford Not To"). The Rand study also demonstrates the economic benefit of prison education to the state.

which, in turn, increases one's likelihood of staying out of prison once released. Indeed, many policymakers and legislators view prison education solely in the context of workforce development. However, the question remains, "Why offer education to those serving life sentences without the possibility of parole who, according to the state, will never enter the workforce?" Oklahoma Baptist University strongly believes *all* incarcerated individuals should be offered the opportunity to earn a college degree. This is an extension of the university's mission. A Christian liberal arts education seeks not only to inform the mind and equip with skills but to transform one's life. It is "education with a soul," as our president is fond of saying. It is education that not only does something *for* a person but also does something *to* that individual, which can be argued is the far greater outcome.

The Greeks are typically credited with birthing liberal arts education (although a case can be made the genesis existed far earlier).[2] The state needed good citizens. Thus, the primary objective of education was designed to shape one's character for civic virtue. Students were taught by pedagogues who "were more than mere tutors of information; they prepared young men to become leaders whose skill sets moved beyond the practical trades, allowing them to deal with civic matters that required more abstract thought and focused reflection. These children of free citizens undertook learning that was directly connected to their citizenship status."[3] This education equipped individuals to enrich their respective communities. The communities of the incarcerated may not look like the communities in which you or I reside. They are enclosed by high walls and fences and isolated from neighboring communities. Yet, they are communities in and of themselves. Should not residents of those communities, i.e. incarcerated men and women, be offered an education which will equip them to improve the quality of life in *their* communities? The answer is a resounding "Yes!" Therein lies the value of a Christian liberal arts

---

2. Henry, "Christian Pursuit of Higher Education," 6–18.
3. Fant, *Liberal Arts*, 24.

education to the incarcerated, even those serving life sentences without a chance for parole.

Such community change is not merely a vision or desire. We are seeing it take place through men like these who are sharing their stories with you. Their Christian liberal arts education has liberated them from the bondage of narrow and, oftentimes, erroneous thinking to pursue truth, to focus on others rather than themselves, and engage their community with intentionality and purpose. Their stories are tales of trepidation and courage, failure and success, aimlessness and purpose, disappointment and affirmation, self-doubt and value. They are stories of transformed lives that are inspiring and leading their neighbors to live better.

The essays that follow are written by men who have experienced transformational learning. They are members of the senior class approaching graduation. They present their stories as testimonies to the transformative power of a Christian liberal arts education. They share them because they have strong desires to impact others with their stories of change. We hope they move people to action:

1. May all individuals, especially those incarcerated, be encouraged to pursue higher education with great diligence wherever the opportunities exist.

2. May legislative bodies always consider the incarcerated population when discussing and funding higher education initiatives.

3. May correctional departments, commissions, and facilities be motivated to create such opportunities and seek partnerships with institutions of higher learning, particularly those who offer a Christian liberal arts education.

4. May colleges and universities welcome such partnerships for their societal value and as an extension of their mission.

5. May professors and instructors eagerly accept opportunities to teach these diligent students and discover their experiences to be among, if not the most, fulfilling of their careers.

INTRODUCTION

To these ends, students are sharing their stories. They also offer suggestions to you, the reader, as to how you can be involved in prison education—whether as a student, administrator, professor, or partner. The Epilogue features an external witness to the effectiveness of the Prison Divinity Program and its success in transforming lives.

I shall be eternally grateful for the opportunity to lead Oklahoma Baptist University's Prison Divinity Program, for it has enabled me to live life with some of God's choicest servants during these past three and a half years and, prayerfully, many more to come. I love and respect these men. I am proud of their academic achievements but more so their love for Jesus and their community. I am eager to see what is written in the next chapter of their lives!

Bruce A. Perkins
Oklahoma Baptist University
Assistant Professor of Christian Education
Director, Prison Divinity Program

BIBLIOGRAPHY

Christian, Sonya. "We Can't Afford Not To." *Liberal Education* 109, no. 2 (Spring 2023). https://www.aacu.org/liberaleducation/articles/we-cant-afford-not-to.

Davis, Lois M., et al. "Evaluating the Effectiveness of Corrections Education: A Meta-Analysis of Programs That Provide Education to Incarcerated Adults." Santa Monica, CA: RAND Corporation, 2013. https://www.rand.org/pubs/research_reports/RR266.html.

Fant, Gene C. *The Liberal Arts: A Student's Guide*. Wheaton, IL: Crossway, 2012.

Henry, Carl F. H. "The Christian Pursuit of Higher Education." *Southern Baptist Journal of Theology* 1, no. 3 (Fall 1997).

PART I

Stories of Personal Growth Leading to Community Impact

A Sheep Dog's Journey

Joshua Benton

PERSONAL REFLECTION

December 8, 2010, was—for all intents and purposes—the day my life ended. You could say that was the day Joshua Benton, son, brother, uncle, father, friend, and veteran died. That day, with great pains, Benton DOC #653854 was born. That morning was the last taste of freedom I would experience outside the confines of a cell and razor-wire fence.

I came from a lower-middle class family. Both my parents worked. My father was an over-the-road truck driver, and my mother worked as a transport tech in diagnostic imaging at the local hospital. At the time, I was working with the county sheriff's office as a jailer. The natural progression from being a security forces officer in the United States Air Force Reserve Command was to begin a career in law enforcement.

Education-wise, I had around thirty hours of college credit at that point in my life. Most of these credit hours were geared toward an associate degree in criminal justice. That choice of career was now thrown out the window. Thus began my new life as an inmate in the Oklahoma Department of Corrections.

PART I. STORIES OF PERSONAL GROWTH

One of the first things I remember in that initial week in county jail was my dad, a man who had not darkened the front door of a church since the mid-nineties, bringing me a King James Version Bible. I had never read the Bible other than skimming through various proverbs. Those first couple of weeks, I tore through the Word, soaking in first just who God is and witnessing his interaction with his chosen people, Israel. Then I came to the New Testament and began to read, for the first time, the teachings of Jesus. Moving through the Gospels to the Letters of Paul, I felt a compelling need to cry out to God and seek deliverance from my situation. I spent hours reading by the dim light coming through the window of my cell door. I began to pray often. One night, while crying out for deliverance from evil, I felt something ripped out of me, and my body physically convulsed on my rack. From that point forward, I was different.

Over the next year and a half, I grew in faith and in my understanding of how God operates. This was aided by a few jailers who were sympathetic to my situation and who were devout Christians. These women helped me see my value in Christ. They provided me with Christian reading material; without them, I would have stayed in a darkness that was consuming me physically and mentally. I should say here that I did not have a substance abuse problem, and by this period in my life, I had stopped drinking. The issue was not related to those material things but was much deeper. I suffered from a spiritual darkness that kept me from seeing God's light. I had cried out to him many times since my tour in Iraq where, in 2008, he first let himself be known to me in a personal way. But now was different. Now I began to call on the name of Jesus. I was seeking deliverance from the murder charge I was facing as well as restoration to my family. Here it is, 2024, and I am still in prison, and my family is all but gone.

In 2012, I entered the custody of the Oklahoma Department of Corrections with a fresh life sentence. I started with nothing yet again, but now I was in a maximum security facility with near 24/7 lockdowns. Eventually, I managed to purchase a TV at too great a cost to my family. This is when I received my first study Bible.

I began to read the word along with the study notes, and this began to bring clarity to obscure things in Scripture. Fast-forward to 2013 and the system transferred me to Joseph Harp Correctional Center. This is a medium-security prison. After nearly a year in a maximum-security unit, I experienced a culture shock.

I had arrived at the "promised land," a yard known for its freedom of movement and recreation. Here I began the early work of forging my road toward becoming an educated Christian. I not only increased my study of Scripture, I found mentors—men who helped me know what discipleship looks like. Then, in 2013, I was accosted by one of these men after I had been found reading a book about Northern Germanic paganism. This interaction drove me away from Christianity. I couldn't fathom a man of God, a man who had a doctoral degree, berating me for seeking to educate myself. I spent a year in these pagan studies and even prayed to these ancient, ancestral deities. While reading one of the larger sagas, the Holy Spirit pointed some things out to me. This led me back to the Bible and back to the same man who shook my faith. I began to serve in the messianic congregation where he pastored. I was eventually baptized by that man on December 9, 2014.

Along the road over the next two years, I completed several correspondence Bible study courses, as well as a class called Evangelism Explosion. This class was my first experience with structured Christian education. I worked within a small group of twelve men over several weeks to learn the basics of evangelism. This gave me the taste for higher Christian education. While Evangelism Explosion had several good elements, it left me with more questions than answers.

My next dip in the Christian education pool was Education for Ministry. This is a four-year, small-group, seminary-like course offered by the Episcopal Diocese of Oklahoma City. It offered Old Testament in the first year, New Testament in the second year, church history in the third year, and wrapped up with an overview of theology in the fourth year. Of the four years, I was able to complete two. This was due to being shipped to Lexington Correctional Center.

PART I. STORIES OF PERSONAL GROWTH

After coming to the correctional center, I was in search of a continuing education program. I found this in a program no longer offered, called Faith Bible Institute. This program is a three-year Bible college. I learned a great deal about Baptist interpretations of Scripture and Bible history from this program and, upon completion, earned a Bible college degree.

Since 2016, I have been what is known as a Benedictine Oblate. This simply means that I am attached to a Benedictine monastery for the purpose of developing spiritual community and growth. This way of life is Christocentric and circles around the sixth-century *Rule of St. Benedict*. This has given me structure and stability to my Christian walk.

The final piece thus far to my educational puzzle has been Oklahoma Baptist University and the Prison Divinity Program. This four-year bachelor's in Christian liberal arts, along with the cohort model, has proven to be great gift from God.

APPLYING MY REFLECTION TO TRANSFORMATIVE TEACHING AND LEARNING

All of the programs discussed above have, in addition to self-guided studies, served to mold my understanding of the Christian faith. They began to work a transformation within me. I began to value educational material that is specifically Christian. I put novels aside and dove headfirst into books about theology, church history, and prayer. I have read books that I would not recommend to anyone and have read some that I have eagerly passed around. In all of this, I have sought the guidance of the Holy Spirit as well as men and women whom I look to as guides in the faith. These guides have shifted from loose contacts to tenured professors via OBU. My outlook and understanding of the Christian faith as well as my place in it have grown exponentially in the last four years.

I view this transformation as a lifelong internal process that is motivated by both personal contemplation of things being presented and social acceptance of those who are presenting the teachings. This has led me to find that the value of highly structured Christian education is not wholly in the content being taught but in the professors who are eager to pour out their love and understanding. This aspect is probably the main difference when it comes to this educational experience. It is uniquely Christian, in that the men and women teaching us approach education from not only career aspects, but more importantly from an avenue of faith. Professors such as Dr. Bruce Perkins and Dr. John-Mark Hart are adamant and faithful followers of Christ. They have shown me an aspect of Baptist interpretation that incorporates the entirety of Christian history in an honest and critical way. This has broadened my mindset and transformed my view of the church. And while there are areas of disagreement, more and more areas of continuity and commonalities are brought to the forefront. This aspect of the Christian liberal arts education presented in the PDP stands out.

My educational experiences leading up to this program did cloud my expectations. I had put so much emphasis on doing things myself that I left others behind. The cohort model in the PDP requires me to come alongside other men and walk with them through the difficulties of this education. I no longer have to carry the burden of understanding and no longer have to figure things out in my own strength. The Bible-based classes are balanced by the general education classes required by the degree outline. Bible studies include learning hermeneutics, doctrine, and the history of the canon, which are all important and necessary for what we are doing. Math, science, history, English, sociology, and psychology are difficult subjects, but they broaden our horizons and allow us to include God in all areas of education or, more to the point, *find* God in all areas of education.

STRATEGIES AND SUGGESTIONS

The model of education we are doing in the PDP may be a proven model in the world, but it is novel to experience in prison. There is such a sense of division that we place among ourselves, usually due to crime and skin color. The cohort model has forced us to live together and, at least for some, work together. This is one practice that needs to be repeated not only in the PDP but in any program seeking to foster cultural change.

The aspect of chapel service for the cohort has been an experiment in taking a widely diverse group—denominationally speaking—and requiring us to worship together. This has been both helpful and hurtful. Helpful in the sense that it has brought us together through the Word and worship experience. Hurtful in that requiring participation for degree completion has forced some to attend just for the sake of being there and making the grade. Chapel is important, but, in an ecumenical mindset, diversification would foster a greater joining together of the cohort. We have Catholic, Baptist, Pentecostal, Presbyterian, nondenominational, Messianic, and a few outliers theologically. If we are to call others to Christ as a group, we need to have an appreciation for the strengths and weaknesses of the various camps within Christianity. Not only from an academic point of view but with an experiential knowledge.

Communion or the Lord's Supper has not been practiced in this cohort, outside of a few small groups early in the program. Even then, we have not done communion in chapel. Nearly all Christians agree communion is one of the sacraments. Historically, communion has been a necessary part of communal worship. Yet, as a cohort, we have not communed together, either under our own guidance or under direction from professors. In the PDP, I see us unifying around the person of Christ as being of utmost importance. Celebrating communion together would serve to solidify this aspect. Denominational understandings aside, the body and the blood are there to unify us.

Our goal is to become ODOC-recognized field ministers. While I understand we are the first class going through this new program, having a more defined meaning and expectation to our role as "Field Minister" would go a long way to getting everyone on board. This has been a sticking point because, as of this writing, we are still a year out from graduation. This has led to much speculation as to what exactly we are going to be expected to do. Having a complete definition with a job description would help not only to get everyone on board, but to get the right people on board. This will allow those of us going through this education to know beforehand what is expected of us so we can implement our ministry as we are going through the program, greatly affecting the yard in a positive manner.

We have been made visible to the yard via OBU headgear and backpacks. This aspect has led to many conversations. It seems like something small when viewed from outside these fences. However, on the inside, we are required to dress alike and any deviance sticks out. Sporting this logo separates us form the rest of the population, but it also allows us to be quickly found when needed.

CONCLUSION

Oklahoma Baptist University has provided a Christian educational experience that has been unrivaled. Yes, as inmates, we can go to our "education" building and pay out of our own pockets to earn a business associate degree. This comes with its own issues of technology and no personal interaction with the professors. However, in this program, after everything I have said thus far, the distinctive element is the professors. Week in and week out, they travel here at their own expense to bring us a quality classroom experience. In this experience the love of Christ is shared with us on an intimate and intellectual level. This has impacted our community as much as any field ministry work we have done. Through these interactions we have grown as Christians, we have grown as ministers, and we have matured as men who now have a purpose. That purpose is to be an effective change agent in the culture around us both inside and outside these fences.

JOSHUA BENTON

Joshua Benton is a father, a brother, a minister, and a veteran. He hails from Bartlesville, Oklahoma. He graduated high school in 2006, entered the Air Force Reserve, and deployed to Iraq in 2008.

PART I. STORIES OF PERSONAL GROWTH

He is now a lifer in the Oklahoma Department of Corrections. He is a student in the first cohort of the OBU Prison Divinity Program. Go Bison!

God's Secret Place

Tracey Brown

IN THE SUMMER OF 2009, I found myself battling depression. Thirty-five years of drug addiction and alcoholism had taken its toll, leaving me with no hope for the future and searching for the will to live. On August 29, 2009, I committed the crime that brought me to prison. It was a hot summer day, and I was floating in my pool drinking whiskey when a guy who owed me money drove into the neighborhood and pulled into a dope-house down the street. So I got out of the pool and went there. I was already buzzed and saw this as an opportunity to get high. Once I got down there, it became obvious that I was not going to get high, so I invited my neighbor down to the house with the intention of confront him about the money he owed. This did not go as well as I had hoped and quickly spiraled out of control. When it was all said and done, I was sitting in a jail cell, charged with first-degree robbery, kidnapping, and extortion. Two years later, I was convicted on all charges and sentenced to twenty years and required to serve at least 85 percent of it. Let this be an example to everyone how quickly drugs and alcohol can destroy your life. I went from floating in my pool to serving twenty years in a matter of minutes. At the time, I believed coming to prison was the worst thing that could have happened to me. However, after only six months, I was diagnosed with cancer and given a year to live.

Battling cancer while facing twenty years in prison felt like a death sentence. Needless to say, God had my full attention.

I have now served fourteen calendar years, and I realize it was God who separated me from the world in order to draw me to himself and heal me. I am now cancer-free and have been since August of 2012. God set me free from the sin that held me in bondage for most of my life. I had to come to prison to be set free. He has called me, and he has made my mouth like a sharp sword; hiding me in the shadow of his hand, he has sharpened and polished me like a steel shaft.[1] Here in the shadows, he has prepared me for that which I have been called. He has hidden me away here in God's secret place for such a time as this. Then he said to me, "You are my servant . . . in whom I will be glorified."[2] God has filled my life with purpose and given me hope for the future.

HOW THE PRISON DIVINITY PROGRAM HAS AFFECTED MY APPROACH TO LIFE AND HOPE FOR THE FUTURE

I believe that, through the vision to educate and equip men in prison to become field ministers, God has revealed to me his purpose and plan for my life. The opportunity to receive a Christian liberal arts education while in prison has demonstrated God's grace to me in a tangible way. This has given me something I can give back. Everything I am learning is flowing through me into everyone within my circle of influence. The Prison Divinity Program has changed my life and given me hope for the future while also providing me with the opportunity to share my experience with men who have no hope. I thank God for the vision, purpose, and plan he has laid out before me. I do not know all the details, but God has allowed me to see enough to step out in faith. I am so grateful for this opportunity that God has given me to shine as a light in this dark place.

1. Isa 49:2.
2. Isa 49:3.

I know his will and purpose for my life is to serve him wherever I am. I have a release date in 2027, and I will be coming home shortly after this book is released, if the Lord tarries. I will be the first person to graduate the PDP and reenter society. I will have a bachelor's degree in Christian liberal arts and one-third of the credits needed for a master's degree. I am fully committed to coming back into the prison system to continue transforming prison culture one man at a time through the power of Jesus Christ. This is my call and his purpose for my life. I am excited to see what doors of opportunity God will open for me in the future.

MY EXPECTATIONS

I am highly confident in Oklahoma Baptist University's dedication to transforming the lives of incarcerated men through the PDP. The high-caliber character and integrity of the people who have been training and equipping us as field ministers is amazing. Many of us are already serving as field ministers and have seen transformation taking place within the prisons by introducing men to the life-transforming power of Jesus. He is turning hearts to repentance. Salvation is having its perfect work, and lives are being transformed.

This is a God-sized vision. We have been strategically placed behind enemy lines for the purpose of reclaiming enemy-occupied territory held by the power of Satan for generations. "For we wrestle not against flesh and blood, but against principalities, against powers, against the rulers of the darkness of this world, against spiritual wickedness in high places."[3] This is a call to war, and those of us who have been called by God for this purpose are committed to laying down our life for this call. Therefore, my expectations are extremely high. I hope and pray that the Oklahoma Department of Corrections is as fully committed to this vision as the PDP and the men who have been called to it are. Together, we will change lives.

---

3. Eph 6:12.

PART I. STORIES OF PERSONAL GROWTH

THINGS THAT NEED TO CHANGE

I am sure there are people who do not understand the investment that stands to be made in the lives of men in prison. Contrary to popular belief, there are some really good men in prison. Some of the best men I have ever known are serving life sentences. The first thing that has to change is the perspective of the incarcerated population. We must come to believe that change in the system is possible. The second thing that has to change is the perspective of those in the free world. We must change the prison system from within, but something must change in the hearts of the people on the outside, as well.

When a man comes to prison he is stripped of all moral integrity, robbing him of any hope for the future. When a man has no hope, he has no incentive to change. A man serving a life sentence in prison can live a life of hope with purpose inside of prison. As field ministers, we will have access to the young men who are just coming into the system or are being placed in disciplinary housing. When they hear men who have been down for decades preaching and teaching hope and transformation, it will inspire them, give them hope, and give them a reason to consider their own lives and futures. After all, many of these men will be released and will be coming back to the communities in which *you* live!

I believe it is time for change, and the Oklahoma Department of Correction has a new motto: "We change lives."[4] If this is true, those in authority need to know there are a number of men who have been called, trained, and equipped by God for this purpose. We are ready and willing to help them make this a reality. Lasting change will come if we work together. Through the combined efforts of ODOC, the PDP, and the field ministers, we will release transformed men back into *your* societies. This is the kind of change that needs to happen!

---

4. Flemming, "Offender Advocacy," para. 1.

STRATEGIES FOR EDUCATORS CONSIDERING SIMILAR PROGRAMS

The vetting process is critical. A high level of accountability is essential for those accepted into the program. This will weed out those who have applied with the wrong motives and slipped through the cracks of the current vetting process. This will protect everyone involved in the program from being compromised by those caught up in prison politics. It also assures that God's money is not being wasted by educating men with no moral compass, character, or integrity.

A high standard of accountability should be maintained, and anyone who compromises the integrity of the program should be made an example of. This will ensure the integrity of the graduating class and guarantee a proper return on investment. This kind of accountability and support must come from, and be enforced by, both the program directors and those in authority within the ODOC. The men in the program will then be able to hold one another accountable. Without proper support from those in authority, the program's integrity is compromised.

You do not play with God's stuff, and the PDP belongs to God. We will all be held accountable for our stewardship of it. We have been chosen by God for his purpose. We must hold ourselves to a higher standard of integrity. God will purge all who are contrary to his vision, including those in authority. God knows what is in the heart of every man.[5]

HOW IT HAS CHANGED ME

The PDP has deepened my understanding and strengthened my walk in Christ. My faith is in his finished work on the cross. His Spirit dwells in me, empowering me to live in victory over sin; presenting my body as a living sacrifice, acceptable to God.[6] The opportunity to obtain a bachelor's degree in Christian liberal arts

---

5. John 2:25.
6. Rom 12:1.

while in prison is something I do not take lightly. Therefore, I no longer conform to the patterns of this world, because I am being transformed by the renewing of my mind.[7] I am a new creation in Christ Jesus; the old man is dead and the new has come.[8] I am renewed in knowledge, after the image of him who created me, Christ.[9] I have peace beyond understanding[10] and I rejoice in the Lord always.[11] Casting my cares on him, I lay my burdens down.[12] I give thanks to the lord because he is good.[13] As I consider all God has done in my past, what he is doing at present, and all he will do in the future, I praise him with a humble heart and a surrendered, obedient life.

WORDS OF ENCOURAGEMENT FOR FUTURE STUDENTS

I would encourage anyone doing time to take advantage of an opportunity like this, and allow God to transform their lives. Prison marks not the end, but the beginning. God will use prison to save and transform your life. He will set you free from a life of bondage, addiction to drugs, alcohol, and violence. He has separated you out of the world to begin the process of transformation. You should take advantage of any opportunity you get to educate yourself through prison education programs. The PDP is an excellent opportunity for you to grow intellectually, as well as spiritually. Don't let prison culture dictate your future. God has a plan and a purpose for your life!

---

7. Rom 12:2.
8. 2 Cor 5:17.
9. Col 3:10.
10. Phil 4:7.
11. Phil 4:4.
12. Ps 55:22.
13. Ps 136:1.

PRIOR EDUCATION

I dropped out of high school in 1981 and obtained my GED. I applied for the PDP for a second chance to obtain an education. With almost forty years passing since my formal education, I knew this would pose a significant challenge. God had already done such a miraculous transformation in my life that I knew this was just the next step in his process. Through God's grace, I am now a senior with a 3.94 grade point average and have been on the president's list for six consecutive semesters. God is no respecter of persons.[14] What he has done for me he can and will do for anyone.

GOD HAS A PURPOSE FOR EVERYTHING

God has given me a desire to encourage men in prison to take responsibility for their lives, own their mistakes, and step into their God-given position of leadership. I am committed to helping them work through the process of healing. As we go through the pain and grief, we learn to process our emotions and allow God to transform our lives. The education I am receiving through the PDP has given me confidence and provided a platform with opportunities to tell men about the life-transforming power of Jesus. Over the last three years, North Church Lexington has begun to spread it roots into prison ministry programs, providing opportunities for us to step into various positions of leadership within the church. This has allowed me to facilitate an addiction recovery program called Breaking Free. This is an amazing testimony of God's grace.

The vision God has given me is one of seeing men set free from sin, which is the root cause of all addictions. I am a recovering addict and alcoholic, whose life has been transformed by the power of God. By God's grace, I have been sober now for over fourteen years, and my life has become an example of the life-transforming power of Jesus. It is through my testimony that I hope to inspire men to pull themselves up and take responsibility

14. Rom 2:11.

for their lives, breaking free from everything that seeks to defeat them and empowering them to step into their God-given position of leadership, point their families to Jesus, and live lives that are examples of his life-transforming power.

My definition of leadership is "a humble servant, who loves people, leads by example, models integrity, receives his vision from God, and has the ability to move people into actions that achieve their objectives." Ministry flows through a personal relationship with Jesus; therefore, a strong prayer life is essential. It allows us to discern the will of God and receive a clear vision. The ability to hear the voice of God comes through the daily reading of his word. We must walk in obedience in response to his voice with uncompromising adherence and integrity.

My perspective is shaped not by my circumstances, but by the passionate convictions and spiritual wisdom that come from the knowledge of God. The Holy Spirit guides me and gives me kingdom vision, empowering me to help others transform their lives. God is using the brokenness of my past to help others be set free, here in God's secret place.

TRACEY BROWN

Tracey Brown was raised by a Christian mother, who brought him to church almost every week, and an outlaw father who taught him how to survive. Tracey prayed to receive salvation at the age of fourteen but soon strayed from God's path by choosing to walk in the footsteps of his father. He began using drugs and alcohol at an early age. After thirty-five years of active drug addiction and alcoholism, he was convicted of the crime which brought him to prison, for which he has served fourteen years on a twenty-year sentence.

BIBLIOGRAPHY

King James Version, Electronic Edition of the 1900 Authorized Version. Bellingham, WA: Faithlife, 2009.

Flemming, Nicole. "Offender Advocacy." About, Oklahoma Department of Corrections. https://oklahoma.gov/doc/about/offender-advocacy.html.

Bridges

Eric Coager

I KNEW SOMETHING HAD to change when I began serving a twenty-two-year prison sentence in 2015. Drug addiction and alcoholism had wreaked havoc on my life. What made it worse was a combination of low self-esteem and quiet acquiescence. I thought I existed in the background of life.

I decided to embrace sobriety. It allowed me to experience and appreciate reality as I never had before. I also signed up for any program with an open slot. Certificates of completion looked good in my record, and they were somewhat helpful. Unfortunately, those programs were only a few weeks long. I needed something more, so I started studying the details of the Bible. The gospel message propelled me into a position of authority over addiction. The truth was that I needed a Savior to deliver me from something more sinister than chemical dependence—sin.

Faith in Jesus turned my life around. Furthermore, it helped me understand God's love. He was calling me to be something greater. Sobriety, facility programs, and faith were movements in the right direction, but I needed a way to put my new life into action. I needed a "bridge" between the gaps of where my life was and where my life could be. Then one day I saw a memo. An Oklahoma college was starting a new program.

A BRIDGE TO THE FUTURE

Oklahoma Baptist University was starting the Prison Divinity Program. They were offering a bachelor's degree in Christian liberal arts. The goal for the PDP was to educate incarcerated students with the intention of affecting a positive influence on the culture inside prison. The idea was to use a peer-to-peer approach, employing the truth of the gospel message. I was skeptical OBU would accept me, although applying to OBU could not hurt—I had nothing to lose.

It seemed like a long shot, but the worst they could do was say no. I took a step of faith and grabbed an application, but I mumbled to myself that college is definitely not for someone like me. I recalled my C average in high school. That was the extent of my educational experience. In addition to that, my family never could have afforded to send me to college. This opportunity inspired a jumble of emotions, but mostly I felt jaded. Nevertheless, I submitted my information and wrote the entrance essays that weekend.

One night, I sifted through my usual pile of mail and noticed a letter from OBU. A whirlwind of astonishment flooded my mind as I rejoiced. My heart raced as I scanned those beautiful words; in short it read, "Accepted." OBU had accepted me into the PDP! Then I paused, questioning whether I would be able to succeed. Though I was on my way to college, I had doubts. Twenty years had passed since high school. I anticipated college courses would be extremely difficult and the professors dry and disconnected from the world outside the classroom. "I will just do my best," I thought to myself as I packed my property and prepared for transport to Lexington Correction Center.

Embarking upon the Journey

I started college in the fall of 2021. Just as I thought, my college courses were challenging but, at the same time, rewarding. I learned I could set my mind toward accomplishing objectives beyond my limits. My professors prompted me to utilize critical thinking skills. As a result, I reflected upon myself and the world around me. I cultivated essential interpersonal skills. I developed a disposition of fellowship with the community, not just with men who were like me, but with those from different cultural backgrounds. My professors certainly were not what I expected either. Each professor brought a sense of real-world application to the classroom. Moreover, they did not treat me like a convict. Instead, they treated me with respect. I was thankful for that. I imagined that this was what it was like to be a regular college student. I was happy. My confidence was developing along with my faith and knowledge.

I confidently made a personal goal during my first year in college to graduate with a 4.0 grade point average. It seemed like an extreme goal initially, but once I received my first transcript, the possibility of accomplishing that goal became real. It all started when PDP director Dr. Bruce Perkins, the professors at OBU, and all the donors to PDP willingly looked beyond my criminal past and equipped me with the tools required for success in life. It seemed that the bridge to my future was my Christian liberal arts education.

Impact on the Community

Dr. Bruce Perkins taught that "the pursuit of knowledge and understanding is the very expression of faith for faith cannot help asking questions."[1] He taught me the importance of having Christian character as well as the value of life. He prompted me to ask critical questions such as "Who am I?" and "What is life really all about?" Through these courses, I learned I was a child of God and no longer a slave to addiction. I did not have to live with that burden anymore. Even though I was in prison, I was free! I wanted to share my discovery of freedom and truth with everyone.

---

1. Perkins, "Nature of Christian Liberal Arts."

A BRIDGE TO THE TRUTH

Jesus said, "The truth will set you free,"[2] but what is truth? There are a few competing theories of truth, according to Dr. Tawa Anderson.[3] The pragmatic theory states that something is true when it works. The coherence theory states that something is true if it coheres to your set of beliefs. Finally, the correspondence theory states that something is true when it corresponds to the way things are. Unfortunately, the postmodern world we live in claims truth is subjective, that there is no "concrete," objective truth. Essentially, this means everyone can decide for himself or herself what truth is. Many people have fallen victim to postmodernism, yielding to a distorted truth based on the unfavorable circumstances they encounter in life. For example, I had accepted the fact that I was an addict as "truth." That was just the way it would always be.

The truth is I am not just an addict or convict. I am a man, a "child of God,"[4] and that is how I want to live my life. Students like me who attend a Christian liberal arts university can learn to have a mindset based on truth, purpose, intentionality, and self-regard. I refused to accept the fringe position of "addict" anymore. When I found this truth, it bolstered my confidence and allowed me to strive, rising above the mistakes of my past.

If you are a prison administrator reading this, ask yourself, "Do I want my population to be full of inmates who embrace the 'prison mentality,' or do I want my residents to exhibit humanity and dignity?" For this reason, it is time to start educating incarcerated men and women with programs like the PDP. Incarcerated persons need truth in order to affect a positive change within prison communities. Everyone needs an education, but not all education is equal. A Christian liberal arts education embraces a beautiful balance of faith, truth, and scholarship. Freedom begins with a bridge to the truth.

---

2. John 8:32.
3. Anderson, "Logic and Truth."
4. Rom 8:16.

PART I. STORIES OF PERSONAL GROWTH

A BRIDGE TO THE COMMUNITY

I was able to start reaching out to the community when I began my first internship just after my sophomore year. Our ministry team went to the Lexington Assessment and Reception Center (A&R) to share the gospel. The A&R is the maximum-security, central holding facility for all incarcerated men entering the Oklahoma Department of Corrections. Men transition after assessment to prisons throughout the state to serve their sentences. Most agree that their days in A&R are some of the hardest. We made it our goal to mitigate those dark days by building a bridge to the community with words of hope.

Our evangelism team interacted each week with men from every demographic of the prison population. Some were dismissive, but the majority were willing to have a conversation. We talked about freedom from sin through Jesus and the tenets of Christianity: loving God, loving people, and living like Jesus. We counseled men with words of encouragement, telling them, "Do not label yourself according to your mistakes, and do not let anyone else label you, either. Your life matters, and God calls you to live above the confines of prison. It is not too late for a change." It was essentially the same message I learned from the Bible and my professors.

Christian liberal arts helped me mature into a responsible man, but it also held pragmatic value as our team interacted with the community with care, compassion, and love rather than indifference, division, and hate. In less than one year, our team led over 300 men to know Jesus at A&R. Those men decided it was time to live life differently. This is my personal testimony after one year of interaction. Now, imagine what could happen if every prison facility in America had Christian liberal arts education programs similar to the PDP.

BRIDGE-BUILDING STRATEGIES

In this essay, I use the metaphor of a bridge for education. One uses a bridge to move from their current position to a desired position.

From my experience, this bridge leads to a holistic lifestyle change, a bolstered sense of self-esteem, and a more effective vocation with greater influence on the community. To continue on the concept of bridges, consider how a builder must think about the kind of traffic that will travel on his bridge before he builds it. Education is a slow, methodical journey fraught with moments of nervousness such as comprehensive final exams. Therefore, I imagine such a bridge as a rope-suspension footbridge. Before I put one foot on that thing, I want to know it is not going to come crashing down. It needs to have structural support. These structural supports can be constructed via the strategies of administrators who allow Christian liberal arts college programs at their facilities, the actions of the educators who participate in the education process, and, most importantly, the continued support of those students who have graduated. Alumni can provide helpful advice to subsequent cohorts as they go through their coursework.

Structural Support

Permission

First, structural support for Christian liberal arts education in prison comes from administration. State corrections agencies and facility staff should trust the process and allow the professors and students to operate as needed. I understand that safety and security take priority. However, vetting a cohort of incarcerated students properly (clean drug test, clear conduct, etc.) will eliminate the necessity to subject such a group to normative lockdowns and shakedowns. College is already challenging; college in prison is uniquely challenging. Do not make the educational process for incarcerated people absurd. Let them learn. After all, hindering a group who demonstrates a desire for a cultural shift for the better may not be the best idea. In other words, suppressing a powerful asset is not a good winning strategy! Administrators: help us help you.

Respect

Second, structural support comes from universities and professors. If you are an educator reading this, there are thousands of incarcerated men and women ready to mature beyond the past and make life better for themselves, for their family, and for the community. Although incarcerated persons have made mistakes, it is not right for them to face perpetual judgment for their life's worst day. It is important for educators to create an environment of mutual respect, where students not only desire to learn but yearn to excel in their studies. Educators, we are normal people. Please treat us like normal people.

Encouragement

Third, structural support comes from the guidance of those who have college experience. If you are a prospective student reading this, after graduation you should consider helping the next generation of students who come in behind you. College is a time for fellowship and building close, lifelong connections with friends, but there are times when you can feel overwhelmed. Having someone who can answer questions and give advice in moments of confusion or frustration may be one of the most valuable resources. Hearing words like, "You can do this," and "Here, let me show you what I did," are relieving. Students, you are engaging succeeding classes as well as the community.

DON'T BURN THE BRIDGES

There is a famous saying, attributed to Socrates, that education is the kindling of a flame, not the filling of a vessel. If education is the birth of a flame, what happens after lighting the fire? Consider how fire can cook a delicious meal, heat water for a bath, and provide warmth in the cold winter months. On the other hand, a wildfire can destroy everything in its path—so it is with education. Students, you only make a first impression once, and being an influencer begins with how you use your education. Make it a goal to use your knowledge for edifying your community rather than trying to impress people with how much you know. No one wants to listen to a smug, know-it-all jerk. If you weaponize your education you can end up burning bridges instead of building them.

CONCLUSION

Educators, you will benefit from being the instrumentation that directly impacts the lives of men and women who need you more than any other students you will ever teach. Society's rejects will become accomplished scholars because you were willing to contribute to the process, which begins in your classroom. You will witness inside out transformation in real time.

Administrators, prison is both a place of occupation and a place of residency. For this reason, college programs like the PDP can benefit you, your facility's staff, and your residents if you are willing to allow colleges to bring in Christian liberal arts programs like the PDP. You will enjoy the transformational experience over time. It seems to me that a student who devotes four years of his or her life to college has some kind of vision for the future. Maybe that vision consists of a career outside of prison. Maybe the vision is to become a positive leader/influencer in the community. Whatever it is, I wager that those incarcerated persons who invest in themselves will not be the type who give wardens headaches and heartburn. Instead, they will be the ones who set the example of what is possible in the lives of incarcerated persons who want to change for the better.

Prospective students, take a proactive role in the rehabilitation process. Learn to let go of maladaptive thinking, and take control of your life once more. Perhaps you can also become an inspiration to friends and family members who are on the same path of destruction. Help put a stop to generational curses like addiction and criminal thinking. Take a step of faith; cross from hopelessness and despair to purposefulness and happiness upon the bridge of education.

PART I. STORIES OF PERSONAL GROWTH

ERIC COAGER

Eric Coager lived and worked as a painter in Tulsa county, Oklahoma for many years. He and his girlfriend, Abigail, are currently engaged to be married. As an undergraduate student at Oklahoma Baptist University, Eric has consistently earned a position on the president's honor roll. He works as a Prison Divinity Program Field Minister, sharing the gospel with men in the Lexington Assessment and Reception Center. Additionally, he plays guitar in the North Church Lexington praise and worship team. He plans to continue his education at Oklahoma Baptist University and ultimately desires to seek a career in Christian counseling.

BIBLIOGRAPHY

Anderson, Tawa. "Logic and Truth." Philosophy 1043: Introduction to Philosophy. Lecture at Oklahoma Baptist University, Lexington, OK, May 25, 2022.
Christian Standard Bible. Nashville: Holman Bible, 2020.
Perkins, Bruce. "Nature of Christian Liberal Arts." Cross-Cultural Ministry 1999: Topics in Christian and Cross-Cultural Ministry Studies. Lecture at Oklahoma Baptist University, Lexington, OK, April 29, 2021.

Worldview and Consistency

Dean Luebberst

LIBERAL ARTS INVOLVE THINKING about how you think, but is a *Christian* liberal arts curriculum necessary? I would say yes. I would say yes from a viewpoint of experience, emotion, and education. Here, I will be leaning heavily on the concept of worldview in Christian liberal arts education.

EARLY LIFE

Three domains of experience shape a worldview: relationships, life events, and institutional experience. Relationships were the most influential in my formative years. My parents were Roman Catholic, but this slipped away—I never witnessed them practice. I like to say I was raised with all the Catholic guilt and none of the theology—dogmatic belief without foundation was the religious volley that set my beliefs to be spiked down in college.

I went to school at a small college in southeastern Ohio. My classes were geared toward achieving a skill set in order to land a very specific career in natural resources. Science classes were rooted in Darwinian evolution and no professor dared to mention the concept of creation. Some professors even mocked the concept of creation. I graduated in 2007, the same year the stock market crashed and no one was hiring. I decided to join the military after finding no employment opportunities in my field. A secular college educated me away from a belief in God, and my military service in Afghanistan during Operation Enduring Freedom cemented my opinion into an angry one. I can vividly remember walking to my barracks during a sandstorm and thinking to myself, "How ridiculous is all this?" Two opposing forces, driven by their conviction that God is with them, have no problem killing one another. For what? Property rights?

My institutional experience was a proverbial cutting of the brake lines that started my runaway freight train of immorality. Popular culture of the early 2000s encouraged people to be who they truly are on the inside. The surrounding culture combined with my education led me to believe I could be whomever I wanted and do whatever I wanted, at whim. My life was a contradiction in that I had no idea who I was, so I changed values as quickly as I could change my mind. I sunk further and further into satisfying the self and developed a mantra for a good life: "The good life is having as little responsibility as possible." I enjoyed the all-American loser lifestyle but worked hard when necessary to get promotions at work. I would take the pay raise and use it to fund my habit of vegetating in the form of alcohol and video games.

I was an atheist and a self-appointed intellectual prior to my incarceration. However, I was a living contradiction. When a person discovers new information, they try to understand it in a way that fits their prejudices. If a qualifying place cannot be found, the information is simply rejected. Loosely defined, an intellectual is someone who makes decisions by utilizing intellect rather than emotion or instinct. How could I furiously dismiss faith as a possible explanation of life when it was something that I did not fully understand? That is the *opposite* of intellectualism. I drank expensive alcohol, listened to national public radio, and hated Republicans. I felt that I had checked all the boxes. Therefore, I was an intellectual. The dirty truth was, it is emotionally satisfying to simply give in to any and all physical desires. Huxley said he chose to believe Darwin because it allowed him all his erotic passions.

I unconsciously felt the same way. I could do what I wanted and feel vindicated. The relationships I gained in college and later the military permitted my agnosticism and my life events gave it precedence. My secular education fueled my thoughts, and my life experience fueled my understanding. This resulted in my thinking the world and everything we know of it was a consequence of natural processes and there could not possibly be a god. My self-centered and godless worldview led me to make some horrible decisions that landed me in prison.

LIFE AFTER A CHRISTIAN LIBERAL ARTS EDUCATION

The recent trend of suspicion toward higher education is legitimate when considering the narrow function of certain spheres of education and the uselessness of others. However, Christian liberal arts education is neither narrow nor useless. Christian liberal arts is not simply studying the Bible and theology. Jesus of Nazareth demonstrated a knowledge of the wider world in his explanation of financial practice, project management, and hiring and firing employees. One would expect the focus of the Bible (Jesus) would only talk about religious things, but he does not.

The Prison Divinity Program answered questions my previous college education did not, such as the problem of ethics. Postmodern thinking has infiltrated many secular universities. The contradictions that exist in postmodernism are startling. Society as a whole would be better in knowing these contradictions. Christian liberal arts education engages both the mind and the heart. Prior to my Christian liberal arts education, I was the center of the universe. I didn't need to learn compassion; I didn't need to learn healthy boundaries; I *needed* a comprehensive moral rehabilitation.

It pains me to make this confession, as I know this book will outlive me and that not only educators and administrators but also my distant relatives will read this. However, I see this as an addendum to the court records many will also read. It is woefully inconsistent that higher education is teaching young people to "live your truth" only to have law enforcement say, "No, you are going to live according to our truth or you are going to prison." The disillusionment of young people is rising and it is no wonder incarceration rates are on the rise. The Judeo-Christian worldview is the most logically consistent worldview and worthy of being investigated.

A warden once described prison as "daycare from hell." I agree with that sentiment, in that the prison community is largely a group of selfish, complaining individuals who think they deserve their way all the time. I am not a sociologist but it would seem that a lifelong pattern of manipulation assists criminals in thinking their emotions are valid and should never be questioned. The Christian liberal arts helped me think about what excites me and why. Dr. Connie Peters helped me grow not only as a student but to mature as a man. An example of this comes from *They Say, I Say* by Birkenstein, Graff, and Durst, which contained short essays that took stances on very controversial topics. Dr. Peters encouraged us to write for and against the authors' opinions on various topics. She was teaching us how to write an effective book review but an unintended side effect was my wrecked sense of entitlement. Christian liberal arts education has turned an emotionally driven buffoon into a reasoning, considerate, and much more thoughtful buffoon.

THE FUTURE FOR PRISON EDUCATION

The stories I shared regarding my corrupt worldview did not stem from a broken home, drug addiction, or abuse. Corrupt worldviews extend from the natural evil that exists in every living human being. Christianity maintains a doctrine known as "total depravity." This doctrine states that no man is naturally good but inclined to evil.[1] Prison cannot turn bad people into good people. At best, prison can house people to protect the public. A regenerate heart and mind come from a power outside of man. Outside of prison. This is not to say prison is of no effect. Incarceration may be the

1. Titus 3:3; John 5:19; Ps 143:2; Job 15:14–15.

"rock bottom" that is used to call the prodigal son home. The call for transformation rather than correction requires a completely new direction in the department.

The new direction for corrections is Christian liberal arts. Dan Pacholke gave a lecture regarding incarceration rates and prison violence at a TEDx Conference.[2] Pacholke suggests it is possible to have environments that are safe, secure, and humane. It is wrong to think that these traits can only exist at the expense of another. He also suggests attempting new strategies to reduce recidivism. These strategies are:

1. More small pilot programs
2. New and better ways to measure impact
3. More opportunities to contribute

Oklahoma Baptist University has worked with the Oklahoma Department of Corrections to provide a safe, secure, and humane environment in which to learn. One could ask, "How is a four-year degree a pilot program?" The Prison Divinity Program is in fact the largest and longest program provided by the Oklahoma Department of Corrections; however, the side projects developed by inmates are not. Since the inception of the Prison Divinity Program at Lexington, the student-inmates have involved the general population in local projects. A yard-beautification project preformed in summer 2023 involved 120 men contributing to maintain unit grounds. This project involved gasoline operated machinery, sharp landscaping tools, and a lot of teamwork. Overall morale on the unit increased and it remains the least violent at the facility.

DEAN LUEBBERST

Dean Luebberst was born in Cincinnati, Ohio. He is divorced with no children and pursuing higher education at Oklahoma Baptist University. He served four years in the United States Air Force from 2010–2014 and completed one tour in Afghanistan with an

---

2. Pacholke, "How Prisons Can Help Inmates Live Better Lives."

PART I. STORIES OF PERSONAL GROWTH

honorable discharge. Dean obtained an associate degree in applied science from Hocking College in Nelsonville, Ohio. He is now pursuing a bachelor's degree in liberal arts from Oklahoma Baptist University with aspirations of obtaining a postgraduate degree.

BIBLIOGRAPHY

Christian Standard Bible. Nashville. TN: Holman Bible, 2018.
Pacholke, Dan. "How Prisons Can Help Inmates Live Better Lives." TED video, 10:22. https://www.ted.com/talks/dan_pacholke_how_prisons_can_help_inmates_live_meaningful_lives?subtitle=en&trigger=0s.

Set Up to Be Used

Joe Sanders II

LIFE IS ABOUT CONSTRUCTION and destruction. I remember as a six-year-old getting my first toy train for Christmas. I was so elated. This was not just some rinky-dink train. This train had the steam engine and real steam puffed from the stack. I waited anxiously as my dad set up the tracks, lending a hand every now and then. Finally, the train was on the tracks. It was a steam engine with several cars behind it. I thought wow! Now what? The train sat silent and motionless. Then my dad looked at me and laughed. He had forgotten the batteries.

Our Father in heaven has given us gifts. As we watch God work, he builds us up in the process and early on we lend a hand. Then he places us on the track and says go out and do what I have called you to do. However, just like the toy train without batteries, apart from God we can do nothing. God sets us up to be used for his purpose.

COMPASSION

Early in my life, others saw much promise in me. Living in the moment as a child, and later as a teen, life did not have a bigger picture. I was a smart and talented kid but academics were not a top priority to me. Sports were my main interest. Doing well in school did not bring me much attention. In contrast, I saw that excelling at sports *did* bring satisfying attention. As I advanced through high school, I became a delinquent—in trouble more often than not. Instead of transforming those around me, I conformed to the culture. As a teen, I wanted to fit in and it seemed that being a thug got more attention than sports and academics. Despite all the dumb things I did while growing up, I can now look back and see God's hand of mercy, grace, and favor upon my life. What God and others saw in me, I did not. I was messing up so much that God tried to pluck me right out the environment I had conformed to by making it possible for me to attend Oklahoma Baptist University via a track scholarship. Me being a young thug, I could not see myself attending a Christian university. I would be remiss if I failed to mention how God still tried to intervene after my not attending OBU.

While sitting at home sometime after graduating high school, I received a phone call from a football coach at Southwestern College, in Weatherford, Oklahoma. He asked if I was still coming that summer and I told him my parents said they did not have any money for me to go to school. The coach told my mother I did not need any money, just bring me there. Again, the hand of God. Favor can get us what money cannot buy. Going to Southwestern College allowed me to see a different world. Few people looked like me, lived like me, or identified with me. The environment was positive: no drugs, no gangs. Church was mandatory every Sunday. I did not want to attend a Christian university, but I was now going to a college where church was mandatory. Feeling out of place, I did not stay there long. I went back to being a thug once I left Southwestern, getting into more trouble. Three years out of high school, I received another full scholarship, this time from Bacone College, in Muskogee, Oklahoma to play football. Talk about set up. Of course, I squandered it by thinking the street life was more important. One year later, I ended up in prison, where I have since stayed for nearly eighteen years. Here, I am in an environment where the majority of the people are like me. Lots of them look like me and identify with me. Here, the need for transformation is dire.

Ultimately, God is in control. I tell myself God said, "OK, now since I have your attention, follow me." Why do I say that? While sitting in my cell tired and weary at wit's end, God sent a knock on my cell door. The man standing at the door had an application in his hand for the Prison Divinity Program. I thought to myself, OBU again! I took the opportunity and thank God, I was accepted. "Then he will restore your fortunes, have compassion on you, and gather you again from all the peoples where the Lord your God has scattered you."[1] God had seen my desire to know him and my desire to want better. He had compassion for me and wanted to use me for his purpose.

What I have learned that has had a major effect on me is the compassion God has for his people. Throughout my life, God has seen my situation and, out of love and compassion, provided the things that would help me, leading me to help others. Christian Worldview class sparked my curiosity and taught me to see the world from a different perspective. Education, emotion, and experience shape our worldview. However, up to this point, experience and emotion had been my only shapers. I was now able to get the knowledge that lays the foundation to confidently and successfully deal with reality. I was able to get an education of the heart, which led to a deepening of my spiritual character through God's word and prayer. Through Christian Worldview, I learned to interpret and submit my experiences and emotions to the standard of Scripture. God's compassion on me then began to affect my emotions toward others. Christian Worldview showed me how to view life through the eyes of Christ. I now sought to answer the questions of life. Why I am here? What is my purpose? Christian Worldview taught me we are to engage the world spiritually with conviction, compassion, and courage.

Being overcome by God's compassion caused me to pray and seek God more, asking that he allow me to see people as he sees them. I prayed, "God, move on my heart in order that I may

1. Deut 30:3.

show people compassion and love them as you do." Oftentimes, we see a person's situation and we have sympathy for them, but that is as far as it goes. Yet still after all the compassion God has shown me, I am still in need of more. This personal need for more compassion opened my eyes to the reality that society needs more compassion. I need compassion, and God gives it freely, so I have purposed to give compassion and show love whenever I can. This came about first with education and then transformation. "Do not be conformed to this age, but be transformed by the renewing of your mind, so that you may discern what is the good, pleasing, and perfect will of God."[2] Spiritual Formation class taught me that, under the influence of the Spirit, my reason, will, and emotions are renewed and changed. I learned to relinquish my will and accept God's will in its place. Coming to know God let me see his character and how he acted in the world. Yes, God is active daily. My heart began to soften, and I found myself being touched by people's situations and wanting to help them even if I did not know them. Be careful what you ask for. I found myself crying when seeing others' struggles on television and hearing inmates tell stories and I thought, "Uh oh, something is happening inside of me." I felt like a big baby.

I welcomed these feelings but tried to hold back the tears in public. I was witnessing transformation take place in my life. It was not any deep, profound teaching that made the impact. It was simply wanting to see the world the way God sees it and wanting to love people the way he loves them by having a Christian worldview. I learned that taking the time to give God attention would put me in position to be aware of people's needs and be available to help them. Early on in life I needed and sought attention, now God bade me seek him first.[3] All along, I had God's attention. It was just that I did not know him to give him the attention that he was due. I learned in Christian Worldview that my understanding of reality pulls me toward the future; it is the same with one's worldview. I learned that the foundation of my worldview is based on what I deem is real. I

2. Rom 12:2.
3. Matt 6:33.

knew God was real and existed in all things, so I allowed Christ to be my foundation. I gained a rational set of beliefs, which allowed me to couple faith with reason, leading to a richer, deeper, more holistic view than that provided by reason alone.

Going through the PDP allowed me to see the need for a change of heart and the renewal of my mind. Without these changes, I could not see people as God sees them and have the compassion necessary to meet a need in their lives. In order to be a positive influence in the lives of others I needed to be a man after God's own heart. I was able to see my own brokenness for once. For me to be able to lead others, I had to begin to repair my own life. Taking the Mind of Christ class taught me to "adopt the same attitude as that of Christ Jesus,"[4] by developing the characteristics of a Christlike mind. I had to become alive, that is, set my mind on the Spirit, which is life and peace. Like the train without batteries, dead on the tracks, I was dead spiritually. I was in need of a spiritual awakening. I also needed to become single-minded. This meant being purely devoted to Christ. Once the train is on the tracks it cannot deviate from its course. With my developing a devotion to Christ, he became my center and foundation. I no longer allowed my mind to be led astray and was able to pay attention to Christ—his commands, his person, and his ways. I was able to stay on course. The Holy Scriptures became the tracks that now guided me through life. "Your word is a lamp for my feet and a light on my path."[5] This class also taught me to be responsive to God. What do I mean by being responsive to God? To understand his word and be sensitive to the Holy Spirit. This came with studying his word and praying. This plays a major role in transformational leadership. In order to lead and be a positive influence, one must be able to excel in following.

Christian Worldview class allowed me to see how Jesus interacted with humanity. Jesus took to the streets, engaging the world with conviction, compassion, and courage. I learned that when it comes to engaging the world, one goal is penetration. We must penetrate and change the world all the while glorifying God as

4. Phil 2:5.
5. Ps 119:105.

Christ did. I learned that the way we engage the world is related to the way we view the world. This newfound compassion allowed me to see others in need physically, spiritually, and emotionally, and be compelled to act on their need. No longer was I afraid to approach someone and try to lend a helping hand anyway I could. As a leader in my church, education does play a role when it comes to leadership and discipleship meetings. The men attending the meetings always ask me to give them something that I have learned while attending OBU. Christian Leadership taught me that we must build relationships. Building these relationships outside of church has led to a growth in our church. By our investing in people, they feel a genuine love and care that draws them in and provides opportunity to be able to influence them.

The change of heart I received has played the biggest role in me reaching out to the community in which I live now. With a hard heart and no compassion, I was like the blind man in Bethsaida.[6] Jesus touched his eyes the first time and people just looked like trees walking around. However, with a second touch, the man's sight was restored. Similarly, people were no longer just an object to me. Greeting a stranger with extended hand and a smile goes a long way. It opens the door for conversation, and once that happens, who knows where God will lead the conversation? I am no longer just present in the community but available to the community. From John Maxwell's *Becoming a Person of Influence*, I also learned his six points to becoming a natural nurturer. "We must commit to others, believe in them, be accessible to them, give with no strings attached, give them opportunities, and lift them to a higher level."[7] This lines up with the biblical principle of loving your neighbor as yourself.[8] Also, God so loved the world that he gave. Out of our love for others, we are to give. We are to put others first. This principle falls in line with the biblical principle, esteem others higher than ourselves. We do this effectively with love and compassion.

6. Mark 8:22–26.
7. Maxwell and Dornan, *Becoming a Person of Influence*, 54.
8. Matt 19:19.

LEADERSHIP

Christian Leadership class is another area in which education has played a vital role in my life. Dealing with transformational leadership, I learned that it could be constructive or destructive. I learned that to model Jesus is to practice the foundation of leadership. In Mark 6 the people questioned, "Is not this the carpenter, the son of Mary?"[9] The Greek word used for carpenter here is τέκτων (pronounced "tekton"), meaning builder and craftsman. God called me to build people up and build up communities. Being an effective transformational leader first, I must allow God to transform me inside and out. Pastor Tony Evans challenges us "to accept and implement the responsibility handed to us by the Creator. He challenges us to honor God in all we do and be Christ like-minded. He challenges us to personal growth and as we rise as kingdom men to reach down and pull others up in the process."[10] I will add to that and say that, as we are reaching down, we must be reaching up to God in order to be successful in our leadership. This is what transformational leadership looks like.

As kingdom men, we are to influence culture, politics, entertainment, and more in a positive way. This is the exact reason professors have invested their time in us here at Lexington through OBU: that we might positively change the culture, prison politics, and be the kingdom men in this environment to help others awaken and rise up. Transformation is a lifelong process. I am excited to be learning how to be a godly leader that will make a positive change in my life and others.

Jesus did not call the cream of the crop to follow him, but rather the lowly and average. What did that mean to me? That meant God sees value in all people. At a time when I saw no value in myself, God said I am his beloved. In prayer, I asked God to show me my purpose and he took my gifts and talents and put them to use for his glory. I am learning that God has always called men to intervene on behalf of a dying world. Ezekiel 22:30 says, "I

---

9. Mark 6:3.
10. Evans, *Kingdom Men Rising*, 2.

searched for a man among them who would repair the wall and stand in the gap before me on behalf of the land so that I might not destroy it, but I found no one."[11] Kingdom men put their faith into action and move on behalf of God and the world. Christ displayed this at the highest level. He came to a dying world to bring healing and restoration. He taught the disciples and instilled in them his vision, which allowed them to carry out his plan after he rose. I have learned also that having a vision is very important because it motivates and provides energy, encourages people to step out in faith, and gives people direction and gets their attention. When people see your vision, they are willing to join in and contribute. Most importantly, I learned it is not my vision but God's vision that I want to bring forth.

My educational journey has been a more spiritual experience than anything else has. I was able to tap in spiritually by going through Spiritual Formation and the Mind of Christ classes. Being Holy Spirit-led and able to walk in Christ has put me in position to follow his lead. Just as the steam engine powers the train, I must allow Jesus' words and the Holy Spirit to empower me. This type of journey has led me to be a mentor to older and younger men. More importantly, it has allowed me to be a leader to the people whom I adapted to as a young man early in life. It is a good feeling when others look to you as a positive leader and you see that hope is in their hearts. It is even greater when they give their lives to Christ as a few have done. When they begin to see you as someone who genuinely cares, that opens the door to get close to them. People do not care what you know until they know that you care.

What does transformational leadership look like? It began with me recognizing the inadequacies in myself and looking into the word of God, allowing him to give correction. Pride was an area that I made a point of emphasis. Pride comes before the fall and I had fallen far enough to know that in order to rise up I needed to be as humble as Jesus is. At the heart of Jesus' leadership was the kingdom of God. His leadership was not in a vacuum. "Jesus' leadership operated in a real world, among real people with

11. Ezek 22:30.

real problems, and showed a new reality has come. Jesus' leadership brought a higher standard, a deeper reality, and a stronger power."[12] Everything Jesus did during his ministry he did to secure a foothold, which would fulfill his long-range strategy to reach the whole world. This is why we can look to Jesus to become a transformational leader. What he did was practical and applicable. Leighton Ford called this "leader as strategist" in his book *Transforming Leadership*.[13]

As a leader, displaying the qualities of Christ are important because that is what will draw people and allow them to trust me and follow me. Looking back, that moment when I asked God to allow me to see people how he does and have compassion as he does was the beginning of my leadership journey. To me, compassion and love go hand in hand. How can one lead without a love for humanity in their heart? Without compassion and love, our leadership will lead to destruction. Ford also spoke about leaders being constructive and destructive. A heart for God and people is how to avoid falling into becoming a destructive leader. Having a heart for God, we will be less likely to compromise our values, character, and authority.

Learning to model Jesus' character has led to me being a better leader in church. Before, I would avoid those who were different, those who represented hate toward my race, and those whose sexual preference I did not agree with. Thank God for his love and compassion as well as for softening my heart and allowing me to see Jesus at work when he walked the earth. I cannot lead with a discriminatory view. One area of community growth has been in the church. Our motto is "where everybody is somebody." I believe the growth is attributed to the love and compassion shown to the men on the yard. Luther said in his book *The Freedom of the Christian*, "As Christians we are free, subject to nothing or no one . . . A Christian is a dutiful servant, subject to everyone."[14] To me, this

---

12. Ford, *Transforming Leadership*, 55.
13. Ford, *Transforming Leadership*, 55.
14. Luther, *Freedom of the Christian*, 1.

means that, although I can do what I want, I must be dedicated to doing the will of God.

STRATEGIES AND SUGGESTIONS

What I have learned through the PDP in regard to Christian leadership and church planting is that everything starts with a vision. A vision came to those who saw a need to fulfill a calling God gave them. This vision was to build up men in prison to be world changers, starting with the environment we are in at this moment. Becoming a transformational leader, we are to model, motivate, mentor, and multiply. Specifically, we are to model integrity. Integrity allows people to trust us and opens the door to relationships. When motivating others, a transformational leader nurtures, has faith in, listens to, and understands other people. What does it mean to nurture others? According to John Maxwell, it is to feed people with encouragement, hope, security, and recognition. It boils down to having genuine concern for others. The key to nurturing is not to allow people to become dependent on us. In nurturing, love is the bridge to connection that makes room for a successful future.

A mentor enlarges, navigates, connects, and empowers other people. As we mentor people, we help them navigate by identifying the destination and having them grab hold of the vision to reach the destination. Navigation requires us to listen to people. Once we know people, we can plot the course. It is, in a sense, being a GPS for them. Most people are confident when using their GPS. Similarly, we are to instill confidence in them. Mentors ultimately empower people. Empowering others allows us to work with and through them. It allows people to reach their highest levels in personal and professional development. Empowering people increases your influence because it also influences all the people they influence.

Looking back at my childhood on that Christmas morning, the excitement I experienced while my dad put together that train has become a foreshadowing. I now watch in amazement as my Father in heaven has set me up to be used by him, giving me an education, filling me with precious cargo and gifts, and placing me on the tracks of life to lead, meet the needs of our world, and reproduce other leaders to affect the world in a positive way. Can you see God's hand in your life trying to set you up to be used for his purpose? God showed up at my door with an opportunity to further my education at the age of thirty-six. I never would have thought that, three years later, a Christian liberal arts program would give me the tools to be a better man and have a heart for all people.

KEYS TO BEING A PERSON OF POSITIVE INFLUENCE

Through what I have learned in the PDP, I have come to believe that transformation is the biggest need we have, both in this place and in the world. This begins with rethinking how we think.

I believe we should study the characteristics of Christ and then allow our minds to develop those same characteristics. As a man thinks in his heart, so is he.[15]

Next, we should put into practice those characteristics. As we observe Christ through the word of God, we see him work.

After careful observation of Christ and putting into practice what we have learned, we then join Christ in his work.

In order for transformation to take place, we must be submitted to the will of God and seek to draw closer to Christ daily.

Only God can transform us into the leaders and people he has called us to be. It is up to us to be open, willing, and obedient to his plans and call on our lives. Gods plans for our lives are good, not evil. His plans are that we prosper.

Throughout the transformation process, God is setting us up to be used for his purpose and his glory. The Builder shows us how to build, at the same time he is building us up, and then he sends us to build up the world around us. Ultimately, it is not the fruit of our work that will cause us to change prison culture and the world, but getting to the root of the problem, which is the heart.

---

15. Prov 23:7.

PART I. STORIES OF PERSONAL GROWTH

JOE SANDERS II

Joe Sanders II was born to Earlene and Joe Sanders Sr. in Fort Benning, Georgia. He is the youngest of four children. He grew up in Redbird, Oklahoma, and graduated from Porter High School in Porter, Oklahoma. He has an associate degree in pastoral ministries from the International Christian College and Seminary. He has three children and one grandchild. He has written and produced thirteen Gospel rap albums with over 700,000 streams and downloads. He is currently a music minister at the Divine Wisdom Worship Center in Lexington, Oklahoma.

BIBLIOGRAPHY

Christian Standard Bible. Nashville: Holman Bible, 2018.
Evans, Tony. *Kingdom Men Rising*. Bloomington, MN: Bethany House, 2021.
Ford, Leighton. *Transforming Leadership*. Downers Grove, IL: InterVarsity, 1991.
Luther, Martin. *The Freedom of the Christian*. Edited and translated by Adam Francisco. Irvine, CA: 1517, 2020.
Maxwell, John, and Jim Dornan. *Becoming a Person of Influence*. Nashville: Thomas Nelson, 1997.

Trash or Treasure?
A Discourse on the Value of Christian Liberal Arts Education Among the Incarcerated Population

Aaron Weiland

INTRODUCTION

UNDERSTANDING THE VALUE OF Christian liberal arts education, particularly in the context of incarceration, begins with understanding the biblical concept of restoration. The overarching story of the Bible teaches that God created human beings with honor and dignity as his image-bearers in the earth; sin corrupted God's original design for humanity, and now God is actively restoring the human race and all creation back to his original, glorious design. This cycle of creation, fall, and restoration describes the universal human story, highlights the special value of a Christian liberal arts education, and provides clarity of purpose for correctional institutions.

My story fits within that framework as a mere testimony of the restoration I have experienced through the Prison Divinity Program in the Oklahoma Department of Corrections. Sharing some of the insights I have discovered along the way, I pray this project serves to mitigate the trend of mass incarceration by encouraging investment in the restorative purpose of God toward the most broken segment of our population.

If restoration defines the purpose of corrections, then restoration must characterize the practice of corrections. Here, hoping to make a positive difference toward meaningful criminal justice reform, I humbly offer personal testimony, personal insights, and practical steps toward that end.

MY EDUCATIONAL JOURNEY

The Downfall

The great shift in my educational journey occurred in the year 2000, during my junior year of high school. The bell rang, which signaled the end of eleventh grade English for the day. As an at-risk student with an unstable home life and a growing drug addiction, the end of class was always my favorite part. Shuffling out the door on my way to the next dreaded lecture, I heard Mr. Goodwin's articulate, baritone voice call my name.

"Mr. Weiland," he bellowed, as he peered over the top of his glasses and summoned me to his desk with one authoritative finger. Little did I know that he was about to open my young eyes to an entirely new realm of possibility. As I cautiously arrived at his desk, he seemed to invoke every ounce of condescension available to him as he brazenly suggested, "Why don't you stop wasting my time and your time and everyone else's time and just drop out already?"

Initially, I was shocked at the suggestion. However, he seemed to have an excellent point. I had never even imagined such a possibility before that day. Nonetheless, the more I thought about it, the more sense it made, and ultimately, as I look back on the past, I remember that day as the beginning of the end of my high school education. Of course, that may have been the fated trajectory of my journey anyway. However, the fact remains; I did not return for my senior year.

Education held no great place of importance in my life for twenty years afterward. It seems I always equated the whole concept of education with accumulating information for the purpose of job preparation. Therefore, with that paradigm, especially in today's age of information availability, formal education held little value to me. Moreover, an essential lifetime of incarceration, which began at eighteen years old, ensured that job preparedness would not factor into my life story.

The Turnaround

The social unrest of 2020 served as the catalyst that sparked within me a desire to pursue a higher level of education. I have been a Christian since the beginning of my incarceration in 2001. Therefore, my faith plays a vital role in the way which I view and approach life. Moreover, my understanding of the Christian faith emphasizes the importance of being salt and light[1] in the midst of a dark and dying world. More specifically, I understand this to mean being a person of influence and illumination in caring for the needs of one's community.

Witnessing the frustrations and divisions of the American people, I recognized a general inability among much of humanity to assess critical situations and communicate meaningful solutions. I saw hurting people unable to constructively express themselves and seemingly powerless to change their unfortunate circumstances. Thus, I developed a strong desire to bring healing and change to the social injustices of our world.

However, I also realized that I myself did not possess the critical thinking or communication skills necessary to provide real solutions. Therefore, I too was no better equipped than anyone else to act upon the desire for change in a significant way. Moreover, my incarceration rendered the opportunity for higher education impossible for me at the time. Nonetheless, the social unrest of 2020 prompted me to begin praying for an opportunity to obtain a

---

1. Matt 5:13–16.

college education in order to be better equipped to minister to the great social needs of our world.

The Path Forward

Weeks of prayer culminated in the facility chaplain, Jeff Laird, approaching me one day with an application for an unheard-of, new college program for prisoners that he excitedly said I "have to do." The PDP, offering a bachelor of arts degree in Christian studies for the purpose of transforming prison culture, perfectly provided the opportunity I sought, and I knew immediately this program was the path forward for me.

While interviewing for the PDP in 2020, Dr. Bruce Perkins introduced me to a type of education that I had never previously imagined. A Christian liberal arts education, he explained, is not exactly intended to prepare one for employability. Rather, a Christian liberal arts education is intended to expand one's thinking capacity and shape one into a certain kind of person. This novel idea of cognitive development and personal transformation instantly piqued my interest and consequently opened the door for a revolutionary new understanding of and appreciation for the entire concept of college education.

Personal Impact

Since being accepted into the PDP, both the intention of a Christian liberal arts education and my personal intention of becoming a difference maker in the world have been and are being radically fulfilled. As I begin my senior year, this experience has imparted to me a greater sense of life purpose and responsibility concerning my role in the overall human story; it has cultivated within me a more holistic thought process and perspective of life, and I have gained increased communication skills by which I am better equipped to exchange, develop, and implement ideas.

TRASH OR TREASURE?

MY APPROACH TO TRANSFORMATIVE TEACHING AND LEARNING PRACTICE

Life Purpose

Life purpose seems to be one of the most significant issues in our world today. The general rejection of absolute truth (and consequently God) has resulted in a society with no sense of life purpose beyond one's own thoughts, feelings, and ambitions. Personally, I grew up with a quintessential postmodern worldview, which Dr. Tawa Anderson described as the contemporary idea that truth is merely "a matter of personal or social belief."[2] Although I certainly would not have used those words, I had no real conception of God other than as some type of nursery rhyme character, no real conception of absolute truth other than my personal experiences, and no real conception of life-purpose other than seeking to fulfill the desires of my own heart. Therefore, I lived a self-centered existence purposed by intoxicant stimulation, sexual gratification, monetary infatuation, and popular acclamation. Understandably, it did not take long until that manner of life proved completely futile and out of touch with reality.

A Christian liberal arts education, by contrast, has helped me recognize more clearly than ever the way in which my life fits into the greater human story. I am not merely an individual human being surrounded by other individual human beings disconnected from myself, nor is my existence simply a series of random, isolated events. Rather, my life is intrinsically connected to the lives of others, and my story is both a continuation of the past and a point of inception regarding the future. Therefore, I have come to understand the overarching purpose of life in terms of investing in the well-being and dignity of those around me and intentionally stewarding this moment in history to positively shape the reality of those who will come after me.

Thus, a Christian liberal arts education answers one of the deepest questions of the human heart: why do I exist? Rather than

---

2. Anderson, *Why Believe*, 51.

providing mere intellectual information, Christian liberal arts education serves to imbue one's very soul with a sense of God-given purpose that gives meaning to all of life. Therefore, seeking to rehabilitate the broken lives and corrupt souls of the American justice system begins not with the superficial behavior modification or employment preparation provided by common prison programs, but with the deeper soul formation that Christian liberal arts education is specifically designed to provide.

Holistic Thinking

The holistic critical thinking skills of a Christian liberal arts education make the fulfillment of this life purpose possible by giving one the cognitive tools necessary to conceive of realities beyond one's own limited perspective and experience of life. Dr. Perkins described this type of cognitive development in terms of *big picture* thinking. Thus, I have learned to see the world through the eyes of other people; I have learned to integrate rather than polarize the diversities of life; I have also learned to exercise deductive reasoning skills by which I am better able to understand the complex relationship between causes and effects. Consequently, this type of holistic thinking empowers one to become an active participant in the direction of one's own life journey rather than existing as a mere collection of DNA randomly bouncing from one moment to the next.

The ability to link multifaceted thoughts together in a logical and focused manner provides the necessary basis for any type of significant leadership. Leroy Eims, as quoted by John C. Maxwell, explained, "A leader is one who sees more than others see, who sees farther than others see, and sees before others do."[3] Regarding social change, positive desire alone accomplishes nothing. However, Christian liberal arts education prepares one for positive action by learning to think in accord with the complexities and diversities of reality. A thought process limited to one's own experiences and

---

3. Maxwell and Dornan, *Becoming a Person of Influence*, 143.

opinions inherently prevents one from rightly understanding the world in which we live. Therefore, the wholistic thinking afforded by Christian liberal arts education frees one from the self-centered, irrational captivity of one's own mind and empowers one to engage the real world in a meaningful way.

Just as in perfecting any skill or ability, making full use of one's mind requires intentional training and preparation. When properly cultivated, the human brain elevates humanity above every other life form on planet Earth and denotes the very difference between human and animal. Thus, Christian liberal arts education actually enables one to become fully human.

Consequentially, a significant factor of incarceration seems to be an inability or a lapse in ability to link together chains of cause and effect in a rational manner. I found this true in my own life when I committed a senseless and life-altering act of violence against another human being for the mere momentary approval of my peers. Rather than accounting for variables beyond one's immediate feelings or ideas, crime generally seems to stem from a shortsighted, self-centered approach to life that does not accord with the complex nature of reality. Thus, the remedy for the shortsighted, self-centered, irrational thought that fuels incarceration lies in the specific cognitive development provided by a Christian liberal arts education.

Communication

Despite the great benefits of living with a sense of life purpose and developing one's cognitive abilities, these qualities in themselves still fall short of producing true cultural change. The practical means by which a Christian liberal arts education serves to empower one to become an agent of community impact lies in the communication skills afforded by this form of education. Instilling life purpose shapes one's motives. Effecting cognitive development enhances one's abilities. However, communication holds the key to transferring the ideas and desires within one's self to real-world application.

PART I. STORIES OF PERSONAL GROWTH

Christian liberal arts education has helped me better appreciate the power of words. Studying the history and literature of Western civilization (the major focus of Christian liberal arts education), I have come to realize that the written and spoken words of successive generations of Christ-followers have largely formed our society as we know it today. Rather than empty expressions of thought or feeling, words shape the reality of the world in which we live. Therefore, Christian liberal arts education teaches one how to exercise language in a clear, focused, and intentional manner. These skills allow rational exchange of ideas by learning to better understand the expressions of others and to better express one's self. Thereby, Christian liberal arts education empowers one to assume an active role in the formation and development of not only one's own life journey but also the human community.

Christian liberal arts education begins by developing one's use of words from mere disjointed expressions of thought or feeling to clear exchange of information. However, the pinnacle of these communication skills lies in making the great leap from clearly exchanging information to intentionally and effectually utilizing language to instill a particular thought or elicit an intended response in one's listeners. This powerful tool, once understood and harnessed, enables one to transfer the life-purpose and wholistic thinking of Christian liberal arts education into the hearts and minds of others in a way that then moves them to action in their own lives. Thus, these skills provide the effective means to multiplying God's restorative purpose amongst the incarcerated population and becoming a true difference maker in the world.

PRACTICAL STRATEGIES FOR COMMUNITY IMPACT

1. Equipping incarcerated men with the sense of life purpose, cognitive development, and communication skills afforded by a Christian liberal arts education empowers these men to become agents of positive change in the families and

communities most plagued by the scourge of crime and mass incarceration. We influence broken families and communities by equipping the absentee fathers, brothers, and sons of those families and communities to become the male leaders their households need them to be.

2. Employing Christian liberal arts educated men in key positions (recreation, education, chapel) in prison influences the culture of the yard by intentionally promoting the physical, mental, and spiritual development of the population.

3. Faith-based housing units provide opportunity to gain enhanced relational skills by learning to work through the basic issues of everyday life in a positive and productive manner.

4. Involvement with churches outside the prison system builds social support networks that enhance both the investment inside the prisons and the possibility of success upon reentry into society.

5. The most basic element of community impact in prison is the freedom for residents to move, gather, and exercise leadership (this requires a combination of trust and accountability between prison residents and prison administration).

In these ways, we may begin to fulfill God's purpose of restoration through the process of incarceration, and prison may become a place more akin to a hospital for broken lives than a landfill for society's garbage. The question is, is that our desire?

AARON WEILAND

Aaron Weiland is a Christian man who has spent the entirety of his adult life incarcerated. He is seeking a bachelor of liberal arts degree in Christian studies. He hopes to gain the cognitive and social tools necessary to contribute a positive influence to the world. Specifically, he hopes to help others find healing and restoration in their lives through mentoring, role modeling, and teaching God's truth. The Bible is his greatest passion in life and his life purpose is to pass it on to the next generation.

BIBLIOGRAPHY

Anderson, Tawa. *Why Believe: Christian Apologetics for a Skeptical Age*. Edited by Heath A. Thomas. Nashville: B&H Academic, 2021.
Christian Standard Bible. Nashville: Holman Bible, 2018.
Maxwell, John C., and Jim Dornan. *Becoming a Person of Influence*. Nashville: Thomas Nelson, 1997.

Field Ministers
Equipped to Serve and Prepared to Return

Arturo Welch

PERSONAL STORY

I GRADUATED FROM AN adult education program two years after I should have completed high school. The fact is, school was never of much interest to me. That truth was part of why I came to prison over twenty-two years ago, at the age of twenty-three. I spent the first dozen years of my imprisonment in maximum security housing because I was considered a dangerous inmate by staff and other inmates. I had no opportunity to enroll in education or other self-improvement programs. Yet it was here in prison that I came to realize that it was only through education that I would be able to see any lasting change in the lives of my family, the men housed around me, or in my own life.

    I never would have thought of my life being valuable or education being important if I were not visited by our facility chaplain while I was housed in the disciplinary unit due to my involvement in an altercation. He spent time teaching me, through Scripture, that every human, even a prisoner, has value. He taught me anyone could be redeemed and made new through faith in Jesus. I gave my life to Christ, but was transferred not long afterward due to another incident.

Three and a half years later, I returned to this facility for the Prison Fellowship Academy Program, which I graduated from in 2019. The program manager was himself a former inmate and had been incarcerated for twenty-five years on a life without parole sentence. He took the job and now works in prison teaching men the skills necessary to reenter society successfully. He opened my eyes to the concept that prisoners are more likely to listen and learn more from men who are or were incarcerated like them.

I also participated in the Faith Bible Institute course at the suggestion of the facility chaplain, who was the same man that led me to Christ. God used these two men to help open my eyes to the possibility of changing prison culture from the inside. Finally, God presented the means for me to gain the skills necessary to start working toward this goal when I was accepted into the Oklahoma Baptist University's Lexington Assessment and Reception Center campus as part of their Prison Divinity Program. The vision of the program is to equip us with these skills through a liberal arts degree focused on Christian studies. We are then going to take the skills we learn and incorporate them with our faith in every area of life while also teaching others by facilitating programs, planting churches, and modeling discipleship.

THE VALUE OF TRAINING RESIDENTS

One question I am sure people are asking is why educate prisoners? If I were investing in this, it would be important to understand what could be expected as far as a realistic return on the investment that was made. I can think of three primary reasons: first, the graduates will be in the best position to serve the residents of the facility where they live specifically because they are there twenty-four hours a day, 365 days a year. Second, as better-educated inmates who have shown themselves to also be model inmates, they will be better able to help staff in every area in which they work. Staff will also be able to utilize graduates to help other residents in need of spiritual guidance, calm tensions with inmates, and work in "facility need" jobs. Third, prisoners who receive an education are much less likely to return to prison and continue to burden taxpayers. Rather, they will be better educated, have more skills, and be capable of attaining higher paying jobs and will thus be an asset to the community into which they return.

I personally learned how to write speeches and speak in a professional manner at an inmate-led club that was affiliated with Toastmasters International. The leader of the club took time to invest in me, personally, because as he said, "Someone else helped me, and you will help the next person." I learned leadership principles from an inmate-facilitated class that utilized John Maxwell's book *21 Irrefutable Laws of Leadership*. That inmate was another mentor of mine, especially in areas of leadership and helping others grow in leadership responsibility. The value of their investment in me cannot be overstated because much of what I first had available to offer others was given to me by them.

While the previously mentioned programs were helpful in giving me tools to grow as a person, they did not give me training in how to integrate my faith in every area of knowledge or how to share it effectively with others. However, OBU's PDP is the means God has used to help me learn how to integrate my faith and previous educational experiences with OBU's own rigorous academic curriculum in order to help people through more effective pastoral care. The help I am now able to offer as an associate pastor of North Church Lexington has been greatly enhanced, as I am now better able to highlight God's truth in every class I teach, every sermon I preach, and every man I personally disciple as I guide these men on how to rightly study God's word for themselves.

SERVICE TO RESIDENTS

OBU graduates will be given the title of "field minister" and be sent out to other facilities to plant churches, give spiritual guidance, and teach programs. The goal of field ministers is to serve their fellow residents by helping them grow spiritually and helping them learn the practical skills needed in order to prepare for their eventual return to society. They must do so by teaching the new skills and thought processes they learned while participating in the PDP. The most effective way of doing so will be leading by example and coming alongside to mentor and advise men looking for change.

I go into the disciplinary unit and speak to men about finding hope and peace, while praying for their everyday needs. A few have taken the visits to heart and started attending Bible studies and church services. They have also joined programs to help them start the journey toward a sober life. I have helped others prepare to earn their GED while encouraging them to recognize that attaining it is only the first step toward building a productive and successful life.

I have taken the Activities of Daily Living class to learn how to take care of residents with disabilities and various medical issues. The reason for doing so was to be better able to help men who are in hospice care and nearing the end of life due to cancer or other terminal diseases. This facility has a very high rate of residents with advanced medical needs and they can feel lost, alone, and forgotten due to being housed in the medical unit infirmary. I have nearly died twice and needed extensive medical assistance in my recovery process. Serving these men through their challenges is critical because no one deserves to feel like they are going to be alone when they die. A group of faithful men are always ready to sit with the terminally ill around the clock so they can be comforted by the presence of someone they know who cares about them.

The pastoral care, basic counseling, and courses provided have helped me grow in my relationship with Jesus and, in doing so, have given me greater compassion for others. It was through this program I came to understand the need to specifically minister to the terminal residents of our community. I came from an ugly background and did not want to see death anymore, especially not up close and not when it involves suffering for weeks or months. The greatest help the program has given me in this area, above the pastoral skills themselves, is the understanding that faith is an action word. That means I must practice what I believe and what I preach. Jesus came to minister to the sick and suffering and, as his disciple, I was given the responsibility and privilege of doing so today on his behalf.

I have led a Bible study group for over five years and conducted classes based on material such as *Bait of Satan* by John Bevere, which helps residents learn how to recognize and properly resolve issues of offense; Evangelism Explosion, a training program by an organization of the same name that teaches men how to have effective gospel conversations and provides an overview of the elements of discipleship; *Resolving Everyday Conflict* by Ken Sande and Kevin Johnson of Peacemaker Ministry, which helps men learn how to handle conflict in a way that honors God and brings reconciliation in relationships; *The Heart of a Man* by Malachi Dads, which helps us learn how to have healthier relationships with our children and other close relatives by allowing God to transform our hearts; as well as Breaking Free, a curriculum series developed by Adult & Teen Challenge, which helps us learn how to break free from toxic denial and the addictive habits that have kept us trapped. I have also led small groups as part of Celebrate Recovery to help support others in starting or continuing their journey toward lifelong sobriety.

Service to others in my community means addressing practical everyday needs such as those mentioned in the previous paragraph. I know it is by God's grace that I have received all of the help, mentoring, and guidance that I have had over the years. I feel honored to be given the opportunity to serve others and help build them up as others have built me up. Serving residents by meeting their needs is one of the most practical ways to begin changing prison culture from within and preparing residents for successful reintegration into regular society.

HELP TO STAFF

I have been asked by staff to enter the disciplinary unit to help bring calm to a volatile situation so they would not have to extract, by force, several angry residents. A primary area of need is the ability of residents to intercede between staff and other residents in order to maintain peace in the facility. By speaking to a resident as a resident, we can relate to issues we all face in ways staff cannot. In addition, as field ministers who have proven our integrity, staff will be more likely to seek us rather than handling problems by force. The fact is, I have seen staff go out of their way to talk issues out but the residents would not talk because of how they are conditioned to view authority figures. Field ministers can bridge the communication gap and bring needed compromise and peaceful resolution to many difficult situations.

Staff have asked me to speak to residents who would not come out of their cells or eat because of the state of their mental health and other issues. The reason the staff have done so is that residents have taken me to them and said they want me to help hold them accountable when they wanted to get sober. Staff could have called mental health workers or done a forced cell extraction but chose instead to utilize my status as a resident to provide the residents with help they would respond to. Helping staff means helping with the behavioral issues of residents in ways that bring about positive results for all parties involved.

I have been asked to serve meals and clean the disciplinary unit during lockdowns that involved gang or racial violence. I am able to do so because staff know I will not break any rules as evidenced by the integrity they have seen and the character I have displayed over the last five years at this facility. I have cleaned cells, showers, and the housing unit floors. I have painted the unit, folded laundry, and done various other tasks to make the officers' job of managing the unit residents easier.

At a previous facility, I also helped staff by working at the mental health unit and meeting the needs of its residents on behalf of staff. I escorted residents to the canteen, to the gym for recreation time, and to the education building to working on getting their GED. All of these tasks were entrusted to me, which freed the housing staff to handle other responsibilities. The fact is, because God has changed me and helped me grow in Christlike character, I have been privileged to help others while practicing service and other ministry related skills. The practicing of such skills, as those gained through the PDP, is also helping me prepare for a successful reentry into society.

PREPARING FOR OUR RETURN

The primary benefit gained by investing in prisoner education is that residents are able to prove their readiness to reenter society successfully when their incarceration ends, as demonstrated by their behavior and service toward other residents and staff during their incarceration. Uneducated men who are unchanged in their thought processes will continue to return to prison. This is an unfortunate reality because they will not see any other option than doing what they always have and getting the same results. Consequently, giving them such skills through a college education is a way to prevent recidivism and allow them to practice skills that will help them find meaningful employment upon their release. I believe that their successful return to society as law-abiding, gainfully employed, taxpaying citizens is in everyone's best interests, especially those who currently pay taxes to warehouse them.

Personally, I know I am called to serve in ministry and whenever I do return to society, I will have years of practical, hands-on experience to go with the skills I am currently gaining thanks to the PDP. I tell people all the time that I am preparing to go home and stay home. I am learning skills that will help me get a good job and keep it. I am learning to be responsible, hardworking, and able to complete work before a given deadline. Just as importantly, I am learning how to build and maintain healthy relationships with people who are like-minded and who want to be held accountable for their actions.

PART I. STORIES OF PERSONAL GROWTH

STRATEGIES FOR GREATEST COMMUNITY IMPACT

I believe there are a few strategies that can help field ministers' efforts to change prison culture. The first being to ensure they are given support from the staff at the facility to which they will be sent. They will not be able to affect any real change if they are stuck on their unit or are unable to have access to class time to do their teaching and training of others. This would need to include the process of informing incoming staff of what field ministers are involved in so that there is no miscommunication or disruption in the ministry they perform for staff or residents.

Second, the fact is that it will be necessary for policy makers to rewrite some policies in order for field ministers to do what we are currently doing on a limited scale, such as ministering to inmates in the disciplinary unit (also called "A&R"), which is classified as maximum security. We will need permission to cross some security levels, for example going from a medium unit to a minimum unit or going from a medium unit into a maximum-security unit. It may be that sending some field ministers to county jails to teach men these skills could prevent prison time altogether for some offenses. This may also include field ministers traveling to places where Scared Straight programs are held in order to help troubled youth realize the consequences of their current choices.

Field ministers will also need to be given the opportunity for further education to both increase their training and to build them up for the continued service of others. Continued education will help keep them focused on the mission while reminding them they have needs that need to be met as well. The most effective teachers and leaders are those who continue to learn. Resource accessibility should be considered by both OBU and the Department of Corrections. Field ministers should be considered for training in Department of Corrections courses such as Thinking for a Change, Victim's Impact, Conflict Resolution, and other court-mandated classes. This would allow us to conduct the courses, which would unburden staff workers and enable some inmates to be released, should they simply be waiting for program completion as a stipulation of their release.

ARTURO WELCH

Arturo Welch grew up with four brothers and two sisters. He and his siblings were raised by their mother, but their dads were not around and/or were abusive. His family was poor and moved around a lot. They did not go to church. Arturo has been incarcerated since 2001, when he was twenty-three. However, he has been following Jesus since February 5, 2015. God has truly blessed him since he surrendered to his will. The opportunity for this education is proof that God can change anyone.

PART II

Stories of Personal Failure Leading to Transformational Achievement

He Has Always Been There
Education Is a Blessing from God

Miguel Caballero

BIOGRAPHY

My name is Juan Carlos Caballero Chavarria—or simply, Miguel. I was born August 24, 1983, in one of the smallest villages of Honduras, at a place called El Canton San Antonio, in the municipality of La Libertad, Comayagua. I come from a "small" family, seven in total, consisting of my dad, my mom, two sisters, two brothers, and myself. I am the middle child and the firstborn son of the family. Growing up, I did not hold a positive view about education. I even looked at education as a waste of time. However, something major happened in my life in 2013 that made me realize I had the wrong perception about education.

EDUCATIONAL JOURNEY

My educational journey began in Comayagua, Honduras, Central America. It was there I started the first grade—my first year of education. I do not remember going to kindergarten, but I remember as clear as crystal where I started the first grade. I did not finish the first grade at the school I started either, because my family was always on the move. Growing up, I remember that we lived in many different places, but the one that is most dear to my heart and the one I think of most often is the one we moved to from Comayagua. This place is called El Violin, La Libertad, Comayagua.

In this place, my dad bought a good piece of land, built a house, and cultivated a nice coffee bean field. That piece of property had very rich and fruitful soil. In the middle of the coffee bean trees, we grew banana trees, sugar cane, oranges, mandarin lemons, etc. We had dogs and raised pigs and chickens. My mom had her own garden where she grew bell peppers, lettuce, tomatoes, carrots, onions, and many other kinds of vegetables.

We also had the tallest avocado tree I have ever seen in my entire life. That avocado tree was about thirty to forty feet tall. My siblings and I would run every morning under the avocado tree to get the fresh, ripe avocados that had fallen from the tree during the night. It was like a competition for us. After picking up the avocados, we would run to the house where mom was waiting for us with homemade tortillas fresh out of the skillet. Those were very good times and, for me, there has been nothing like them since.

From El Violin, I went to a school that was about three or four miles north of my house in another village called El Filo. I walked every day to go to this school until I finished the third grade. When I finished the third grade, my parents enrolled me in another school. This time, the school was about three or four miles south, and I had to walk there, also.

It was here in this school, Roberto Anibal Orellana, in La Esperanza, La Libertad, Comayagua, that I finished the sixth grade. In Honduras, finishing the sixth grade is actually a big deal. They held a big graduation party as if the students were graduating from high school.

HIGH HILLS

When I finished the sixth grade, my dad sold the piece of land we had in El Violin, bought a car, and moved our family to another village called Loma Alta—High Hills—where we opened a grocery store. While living in Loma Alta, my dad used the car to go to town, keep the grocery store supplied, and transport people from the town to the villages and vice-versa. He even began using the car to sell vegetables and fruits. To do this, my dad and I went regularly to the city where we could buy fresh fruits and vegetables at a lower price. We would then go to back to town to sell them. We made a good profit this way.

We continued this for awhile until my dad started to abuse alcohol. One day, while drunk, he decided to physically mistreat my mother. This incident, on top of many other previous misunderstandings between them, caused a temporary separation of the family. My mother went to live with her sister in Comayagua, and took all my siblings with her. Only I stayed behind with my dad. In fact, I was the one who drove all of them to the city in my dad's car. This separation did not last long because my mom forgave my dad a few months later. After they reconciled, we all moved to the city and never went back to live in villages or small towns again.

BACK TO COMAYAGUA

In Comayagua, even though we moved to one of the most dangerous and poor neighborhoods in the city, I quickly fell in love with the fast city life. I was a teenager and soon started to think that I knew it all and needed no one to tell me what to do.

I worked at a gas station, a construction company, and even a mechanic workshop, until I finally found a steady job where I worked for about eight years. The owners of this establishment, Marwan Khaliliyeh and his wife, Wisam Saba, took me under their wings. They showed me love and taught me how to work in their hardware store, Ferreteria el Jordan. While working for them, I enrolled myself in night school and finally started seventh grade. When that year ended, I realized I had not passed; I had been distracted and more concerned about girls and the nightlife than the schoolwork.

The next year, I enrolled in night school again. This time, I quit before the year ended. The following year, I did not even try

PART II. STORIES OF PERSONAL FAILURE

to enroll. Instead, I stayed at home to take care of my daughter, Nickoll, so that her mom, Claudia Suyapa Espinal, could enroll. My beautiful Nickoll, who was but a few months old at the time, is now a lovely young woman—twenty-one years old. *She is the best thing that has ever happened to me.*

JUSTIFYING FAILURE

The way I used to justify my laziness and failure in school was by telling myself that education was a waste of time. I was already working and making good money. Therefore, I thought I did not need any more education in my life. In hindsight, I can see I was wrong. I thought I was going to work at the hardware store until dying at an old age. However, I had a rude awakening when, spur of the moment, I decided to leave the hardware store and my country as a whole to come to the USA.

NEW YORK

When I first came to the United States in 2006, the first state I lived in was New York. New York is a beautiful place. There, I worked various positions at Italian restaurants and construction companies. Because of my lack of education, I could not aspire to something better, and my opportunities were very limited. While living in Long Island, I enrolled in night school one more time. I went to school a few times and soon realized that I did not really like going to school.

I wanted to work and "make money" instead of wasting my time reading books and learning. Even though I knew I was going to be making very little money unless I earned some sort of education, I did not want to do all the work needed to finish school and get a degree. I can see now that if I had committed to school and finished my education, my life could have been a lot easier and potentially different.

OKLAHOMA

In 2008, I moved from New York to Oklahoma. This was a big change for me. However, I started to see a pattern in the jobs I took: farms, restaurants, and construction. In my mind, I could not aspire to anything better with the education I had. Still, I did not want to do the work or pay the price necessary for me to better myself. Nonetheless, everything was about to change.

NEW BEGINNING

In June of 2013, my whole life and thoughts about education finally changed. Due to my ignorance, bad decisions, and drug involvement, I found myself in a four-wall cell in jail waiting to be sentenced for a crime I had committed. In that cell, I felt helpless, hopeless, desperate, and completely lost. Feeling that way, I got on my knees and, with a sincere heart, begged God for mercy and forgiveness. The Lord God is good. He heard me and met me there in that county jail cell when I cried out to him. He heard me, forgave me, and saved me.

HUNGRY FOR KNOWLEDGE

After giving my life to Jesus on July 5, 2013, a strong desire for learning arose within me. The book of Proverbs says, "The fear of the Lord is the beginning of wisdom."[1] It is true; after having an encounter with the living God, he changed my desires and views about learning. When I was in Cherokee County Jail, I spoke Spanish. Yes, I could speak a few words of English here and there, but I could not keep up in conversation. I felt odd and lost in translation. To be honest, when people spoke around me, I thought they were making fun of me or were out to get me. However, I had a great zeal for the Lord, and I wanted to share my faith with the people around me. Therefore, I asked the Lord to teach me English

---

1. Prov 1:7.

because I wanted to share his word with the world. I see now that what I was asking God for was a better education so I could be able to help others. The Lord is faithful and he provided me with the means to do it.

ARRIVING AT DICK CONNER

When I arrived at Dick Conner Correctional Center in 2015, I went to the education building where tutors started to prep me to earn my GED in Spanish. After a few tests, they told me I was ready to take my GED. However, they also asked me if I wanted to learn English so that I may earn my GED in English, to which I answered with a resounding "Yes!" To me, this was the answer to the prayer I prayed in county jail about wanting to learn English to share the word of God with the world. The tutors began working with me, teaching me English for about seven months. Then, one day, I received a notification in the mail from the education building telling me that I was scheduled to go and take the GED exam. I went and, to my surprise, I passed it! All glory, honor, and praise be to God! I know he helped me.

After getting my GED at the end of 2015, I enrolled in a school to obtain a bachelor's degree in biblical studies. Since I could work at my own pace, I ended up finishing it in less than two years. Looking back, I can see that, even though this degree was not accredited, God was preparing me by getting me well acquainted with the English language so that He could then bring me to Oklahoma Baptist University to obtain an accredited bachelor's degree in Christian liberal arts.

VALUE OF EDUCATION

Besides salvation, I believe education is the best thing that a person can receive in life. It has been ten years since I started the journey of learning how to be a man of God. These last three years at OBU have been a life-transforming experience for me. I have received not only a Christian education but also a general education, which is going to help me to have a better future in the real world. The Lord, through the faithful and dedicated professors of OBU, has been and is truly equipping me to be successful in every area of my life here in prison, and especially to be successful in society when I get out of this place.

Truly, "[A]s a Christian liberal arts university, OBU transforms lives by equipping students to pursue academic excellence, integrate faith with all areas of knowledge, engage a diverse world, and live worthy of the high calling of God in Christ."[2] This is exactly what I have been experiencing and learning here at the OBU Lexington Campus. Moreover, because I have been applying the principles I have been learning, the Lord has already started using me in ways I never thought were possible. I have been able to lead people to Jesus, baptize them, lead worship, teach, preach the word of God, and even write articles for churches.

The *Baptist Messenger* published my story, along with a message about what the Lord is doing here on the OBU Lexington Campus, in their November 2023 edition. I even made it onto the cover page. In prison? Yes, even in prison. There is nothing impossible or too hard for God to do.

In August 2022, the College Heights Baptist Church board, led by Senior Pastor Bryan Haynes, unanimously voted me into their staff as Associate Pastor of Prison Ministries at Chickasha, Oklahoma. I get to pastor a church even while I am still behind bars. I am telling you that God is good. If we take advantage of the opportunities he places in front of us, there is no telling where he can take us or the things he can do in us, for us, and through us. I believe that if God can do this for me, he can do it for anyone who trusts him and yields to him. God is not partial.

---

2. "Mission Statement," About OBU, Oklahoma Baptist University, para. 1.

PART II. STORIES OF PERSONAL FAILURE

HARD WORK

For me, education has never been an easy task. It requires hard work. Many times, you are going to feel like a failure; you will be frustrated, thinking you do not have what it takes, and ready to give up. There are a couple of things that have helped me as I have been studying over these past few years. The first is understanding that I am not entitled to anything. Education is a blessing from God to me. The second is that I do not have to study; I *get* to study so that I may better myself, have a better future, and be able to help others in need.

INSIGHTS

The insight I can share with you about how to experience success in education is you have to want it. Pray to God to help you. Ask other students for help when needed. Be disciplined. Do not squander your time. Do not procrastinate. If you have time to do your work, do it right away. When you do what you need to do as soon as you can, then you will have time to do what you want, whenever you want. Be responsible and encourage yourself. You can do it. Remember, all things are possible for him who believes in God and in himself.

SPECIAL THANKS

To all of you who support Christian liberal arts education, and education in general in any way, shape, or form, I want to say, on behalf of many grateful beneficiaries including myself, thank you. We would not be able to do what we do and receive the education we receive if it were not for people like you. God is using you mightily to change lives for his praise and glory. You are contributing to the transformation of many individuals' lives who will in turn go and transform others. I am one of those who have been transformed by education and will go to take the good news of salvation to others so they can also be saved and transformed. Thank you. God bless you. To God be the glory.

MIGUEL CABALLERO

Juan "Miguel" Carlos Caballero Chavarria was born in one of the smallest villages of Honduras, Central America, a place called El Canton San Antonio, La Libertad Comayagua. He comes from a family of seven, consisting of his dad, mom, two sisters, two brothers, and himself. He is the middle child and the firstborn son of the family. Growing up, he did not hold a positive view about education, even looking at education as a waste of time. However, something major happened in his life in 2013 that made him realize that he had the wrong perception of education.

BIBLIOGRAPHY

Christian Standard Bible. Nashville, TN: Holman Bible, 2018.
"Mission Statement." About, Oklahoma Baptist University. https://www.okbu.edu/about/mission/statement.html.

A Mountain I Must Climb

Leslie Shayne Smith

PERSONAL REFLECTION

I CAN REMEMBER BEING terrified when I was in kindergarten. I was so scared when my mom would drop me off for school. I would fight to go with her by clinging to her leg. The teacher would have to literally pull me away from her. Looking back, I have discovered why I was so scared to go to school. My parents argued all the time while I was a bystander. When I was seven years old, my parents divorced. This event turned my world upside down. I believe I was afraid Mom would abandon me due to the environment I lived in.

My educational journey got off to a really bad start. When my parents divorced, my two siblings and I lived at our grandparents' home with Mom. Soon after this, we moved into our own apartment. From that point on our life was chaos. The broken home situation impacted my life greatly. This all affected my educational experience. When I was in school, all I could think about was whether or not Mom was going to pick me up. This took my focus off of my classes, which resulted in poor grades. This is when education became what I now refer to as the proverbial mountain in my life.

My grades were so poor that I was held back in the first grade. This only added to my insecurities. Now I was the oldest kid in class, and I was being made fun of because of it. This made me feel very uncomfortable, like I was always coming from behind. When I would begin to feel this way, I would attempt to avoid the work. All of these things led me to act out in class. I became the class clown, which resulted in me being sent to the principal's office on multiple occasions.

I went on to continue this downward spiral, resulting in me getting held back again. This only made things worse for me. The mountain in my way was getting bigger. Now I did not even want to go to school, so I began to skip. I would leave the school grounds and ride my bike through the city area. When I would attempt to do my homework, I would get frustrated and put it away. My attendance was horrible, which led the school district to get involved.

Once I finally made it to middle school, I started to hang out with a pretty rough group of kids who used drugs. Needless to say, I began to use drugs and got involved in relationships that were unhealthy. The last school that I attended was a Christian private school. The school required uniforms, but I rebelled and never wore one. I was sixteen and ready to be done with school, so I dropped out. I never completed my eighth-grade year. I decided not to climb the mountain that stood in my way.

I went on to work several different jobs without much success. I was twenty-one years old when I got arrested and placed on a two-year probation. One of the court's requirements was for me to get my GED. I studied for it and found that I did much better than I expected I would. I can remember the teacher telling me that my grades were above average and this shocked me. After achieving my GED, I did not pursue any further education.

I ended up coming to prison in 2014 with a twenty-year sentence. After doing several years of my sentence, Oklahoma Baptist University and the Oklahoma Department of Corrections announced they would be offering an opportunity to achieve a bachelor's degree in Christian studies. They were going to use this opportunity to train inmates to become field ministers with the goal of transforming prison culture. It would be called the Prison Divinity Program. After praying about it, I decided to apply.

I applied and was not accepted, which was very discouraging. There was a second opportunity to apply; I reapplied and still was not accepted. A third opportunity was presented, but by this time I did not want to get rejected again. You see, I gained a great fear of rejection by this time, and I would typically try to avoid it. But with the encouragement of the facility chaplain, I ended up applying a third time. You know the old saying, "third time's a charm," but this was no roll of the dice. This was an opportunity for me to face the mountain that had stood in my way my entire life. Every time things got difficult or challenging, I had run from the proverbial mountain.

I was so thankful to be included in the Oklahoma Baptist University prison divinity family, but what about that mountain? I found my first semester to be challenging but completed it with all A's. It was the second semester that I found myself staring at that mountain once again. You see, I had learned how to stay in my comfort zone in life, and would avoid anything that confronted my learning insecurities. What I failed to consider when I applied to the program was that I was placing myself in a vulnerable position.

In the second semester of my freshman year, the challenge became more than I thought I could bear. I remember standing up in the classroom and sharing my childhood struggle with education. I admitted to them that I felt like running. I was so overwhelmed with emotion because I felt like that little boy again who failed the first grade. I was facing that mountain once again, but now I was a forty-five-year-old man.

Filled with doubt and emotion, I decided to call my parents, who encouraged me to take this opportunity that God was giving me to trust in him and finally climb the mountain. They assured me that God was healing me of the educational insecurities I obtained during my previous educational experiences. I also received much encouragement and affirmation from my classmates. I made up my mind that I was not going to run this time. I was determined to climb the mountain. For the first time in my life, I was going to face the difficulty head on. If it was not for prison educators offering me this amazing opportunity, I would not have this chance to grow in this area. I am now in the second semester of my junior year and currently have all A's. Now I know that I can learn and that I am smart enough to do the work. I am so thankful that this opportunity was given because it has played a major role in helping me overcome my fears. That little boy finally climbed the mountain.

TRANSFORMATIVE TEACHING AND LEARNING

Had it not been for educators who believed in the incarcerated, I would not have had access to the education I am now receiving. Transformative teaching and learning take intentionality. When teachers believe in people, transformative teaching will happen. Looking back, I don't know if I ever had a teacher who really reached out to help me the way the Prison Divinity Program professors have. The teaching I have experienced these past three years has transformed my life. This transformative teaching has given me confidence and a better understanding of the world.

I have learned how to learn. By this I mean I learned how to apply myself by doing the work necessary to be successful. This has been very transforming for me because I used to feel like I already knew everything. Just because I do not already know something does not mean I am incompetent. Now, I know the beauty is in the learning itself. The education is not for another notch in the belt, but for the knowledge and growth that I will gain. Sometimes, I still experience those old, familiar insecurities when I am challenged with my education. When I do, I remind myself of all I have achieved. To me this is a part of transformative teaching and learning. When you learn *how* you learn, you realize that you can learn anything.

My education has taught me how to do life more effectively. The challenges I have overcome in education have shown me that if I put my mind to it, I can accomplish difficult tasks. When I begin to feel overwhelmed now, I gather my thoughts and begin to consider tactics to get the job done. Instead of running when things get difficult, I apply the learning techniques I have gained. This entire process is transformative. I believe we were designed to constantly be in a state of transformation. When I receive my bachelor's degree in a year and a half, I will continue to pursue my education. I never want to stop being transformed by teaching and learning.

The transformation that has taken place in my life has been made possible because education has helped me improve my everyday problem solving. Now, when I am faced with difficult circumstances, I know I can troubleshoot and probably complete the task. I am constantly faced with challenging situations while serving as an inmate pastor, as well as at work and in my community. I am now able to apply the same principles I have learned through my education to my job. This transformation through education has certainly benefited me with regard to public relations and communication.

I now serve in prison ministry as an inmate pastor, which requires me to deal with the public. I also work for the facility chaplain. Serving my community in this capacity requires me to communicate effectively. My education has taught me how to consider the worldview of others as well as how to take my faith into a diverse world. My particular degree has equipped me to preach, teach, counsel, problem-solve, lead, manage, plan special events, and even conduct funerals.

STRATEGIES AND SUGGESTIONS

For teachers and education institutions who are genuinely interested in making a difference in this world, I highly recommend educating those who are incarcerated. Most people who are incarcerated did not achieve much of an education. About 85 percent of those currently incarcerated will return to society. It only makes good sense to educate them before returning them to their communities. These educated inmates can return to society with something to offer. If they are not educated, they will likely return to doing what it was that placed them in prison. Many became incarcerated by attempting to provide for their families.

Most people who are incarcerated are insecure like I was before receiving education. In many cases, these insecurities led them to act out in violence. Education makes people secure. It gives them a sense of self-worth and value. Not only will educating the incarcerated give them security, it will result in safer prisons. I have already mentioned the fact that the majority will return to your communities. If they are educated, they will uphold safer engagement in their community upon release.

Why not use those with a criminal background to teach the youth of America how to live a healthy, productive life? When the incarcerated are educated, that is what will likely happen. They will have learned from their past failures that there is a better way and, in turn, teach youths how to avoid making the same mistakes. When you educate an incarcerated person, you have done something powerful. You will send home men and women who have overcome some very serious obstacles. When you educate the incarcerated, you are educating mothers and fathers who will return to their families more fit to provide.

I believe that investing in the education of those in prison will be most rewarding. One of the reasons I believe this is because of all they have been through. Most college graduates are younger than twenty-five. With the incarcerated this average is much older. This education means something more to them. They are hungry not only to learn but to make a difference in their communities through education.

Many times, inmates who are serving a life sentence are not given the same opportunities as those with a release date. I suggest that those serving a life sentence be invested in as well. These are the ones who will pour into those who will eventually return to society. It is wise to educate them with the intention of using them to educate other inmates who will return home. Doing this will give the ones doing life in prison purpose, while also preparing those with release dates to return home educated and healthy.

PART II. STORIES OF PERSONAL FAILURE

Education not only gives inmates knowledge; more so, it teaches them how to *do* life. Educators play a vital role in the prison population and the recidivism rate. If the incarcerated are educated, they will be transformed and will in turn transform others. When they become educated, they will not only transform prison culture but the culture of your communities as well. It is an investment with endless reward.

LESLIE SHAYNE SMITH

Leslie Shayne Smith was born in Fort Worth, Texas, and moved to Oklahoma in his mid-twenties. He came from a broken home and struggled with school for all of his childhood. He dropped out when he was sixteen, before completing the eighth grade. He came to prison when he was thirty-eight. He learned how to face his learning challenges when he was accepted into the Prison Divinity Program. He has persevered when he wanted to run.

A College Education Like a Multifunctional Tool

Vincent Todd Ochoa

INTRODUCTION

ON APRIL 5, 2021, I began my journey as a college student in the Oklahoma Baptist University Prison Divinity Program held at the Lexington Correctional Center in the Oklahoma Department of Corrections. Prior to my incarceration, I was an automotive technician, and tools were the instruments of my trade. To me, the liberal arts college education that I am receiving through the OBU Prison Divinity Program is like a multifunctional tool that God has graciously provided in order to prepare me to accomplish the work he has preordained for me to do. Through my educational journey, I have discovered that I am capable of achieving beyond my expectations.

PART II. STORIES OF PERSONAL FAILURE

MY CHILDHOOD EDUCATIONAL EXPERIENCE

I was born in Wichita Falls, Texas, and raised by a single mother who struggled to balance the needs of her five children with her prescription pill addiction, alcoholism, and mental illness. My dad left my mother when I was around three years old, and I grew up without a father. My mom's personal issues would not allow her to hold a steady job, so she depended heavily on having a man in her life, which she found in dysfunctional men with alcoholism and personal issues similar to her own. She married four times and was regularly in and out of relationships with them. Life at home for me was very dysfunctional and unpredictable. My mother would regularly move us kids from one place to another like drifters. Because of this, we never had any real stability. I ended up spending some time in and out of foster homes while my mother would attempt to get her life together after one of her nervous breakdowns.

Due to my family dysfunction and instability, I never did well in school throughout my entire childhood. My home life was so unstable that I remember having to enroll into four different schools during one single school year. There were times we struggled with poverty, and I would have to wear the same clothes to school day after day. Being poor and feeling the rejection of no father made me an insecure kid and gave me a sense of low self-esteem that plagued me into my adulthood. From around the sixth grade forward, I was that quiet kid who always sat in the back of the class—complete with the long hair and rebellious attitude—who was there only because he had to be. I never participated in class discussions and just wanted to be unseen and left alone. Sadly, I had a number of teachers accommodate me in that particular area throughout my school years, treating me like I was as inconsequential to them, as I was feeling inside. The rejection I felt only added to my insecurity and rebellion toward education. When I flunked the first grade, I remember my teacher informing my mother that I had learning and literacy disabilities and would most likely need special education classes to catch up. I eventually spent the fifth grade in a special education class learning to read better and correctly pronounce words due to a speech impediment. I somehow made it to the eighth grade and ended up generously passed into the ninth grade by teachers who I believe felt sorry for me. At the age of sixteen, I eventually dropped out of high school just three months into my ninth-grade year because the schoolwork was just too hard for me and because I wanted to leave home in an attempt to escape the dysfunction. I later learned that no matter how far I ran, I could not escape the dysfunction because it had become a dominating part of my life.

MY PRISON EDUCATION EXPERIENCE

Fast forward nineteen years later and I had reached the age of thirty-five and received a life sentence without parole. In September of 2002, I was convicted for the fatal shooting of a man mutually considered an enemy in the drug world I was involved in. I was then sent to the notorious Oklahoma State Reformatory in Granite, Oklahoma, to begin serving out the sentence. The first thing I did upon my arrival was enroll in the Lakeside High School to try to earn a GED, which I was narrowly able to accomplish. It took ten months of a full day's worth of weekly classes and the assistance of formerly retired teachers who worked in the prison high school, along with two attempts at the GED test, for me to get it.

Now, eighteen years later, at the age of fifty-four, with much reservation due to a lack of self-confidence and a fear of failing and with twenty-one years of incarceration behind me, I found myself completing an application for the new OBU Prison Divinity Program. The application stated that the PDP's goal was to teach and train inmates serving lengthy sentences to become field ministers so that they may impact and cause change in the prison culture they live in. I had experienced a very powerful conversion to Christianity twenty-one years earlier, while I was in the county jail shortly after my arrest, that had immediately changed my life. After that event, I spent the next twenty-one years sharing my faith with others, making disciples, teaching new believers, and preaching and teaching God's word in a discipleship ministry I had founded ten years earlier. I strongly felt that the PDP could possibly give me the training I needed in order to perform more effective ministry, so I completed the OBU college application after a little nudging by our facility chaplain, who informed me that he could not think of a better candidate for the program than me. I did not consider myself a good candidate at all because of my prior school experience and because I had not ever used a computer. Just the thought of having to use a computer gave me much reservation. I was just not sure that I would be able to climb such a high mountain as college, but I knew I would regret not trying.

LEARNING TO RELEASE MY FEARS

My college education began in the spring of 2021. We started with three pre-semester prep classes called an Introduction to the Prison Divinity Program, Preparing to Engage Your College Education, and Christianity 101. The pre-semester work seemed tough at first, especially learning how to use the laptop computer. I was a decent automotive mechanic prior to prison but I was not good with electronic technology. I had never even used a cell phone or played a video game prior to prison. I eventually got with one of my younger fellow PDP students who happened to be a whiz with computers and arranged for him to tutor me in that area, but I was a slow learner and struggled with the computer, which only increased my anxiety level. It was also a bit of a struggle trying to schedule my classes and study time around my preexisting daily activities, and I quickly learned that I would have to schedule my daily activities around my college education instead. My anxiety level dropped some and my self-pride took a needed boost when I received an A on my first exam! I ended up doing so much better than I expected during that short prep period and came out of it with a passing grade in each of my classes. This gave me a sliver of hope that I just might be able to succeed at college after all.

MY "ROCKY MOVIE" ATTITUDE

The day arrived for me to begin the first semester of college, and I still had a low expectation of my ability to do well and felt the work was probably going to be too hard for me. I was not sure I would be able to maintain a decent grade point average, let alone be able to finish. I knew I was not alone in this thought as other students expressed their own worries with me. After patiently listening to me voice my anxieties, Dr. Bruce Perkins, director of the PDP, offered some loving and gentle encouragement, then gave me three simple instructions to follow: show up for your classes, turn your work in on time, and ask questions. He said that if I did those things, I would be just fine.

I entered my first college semester with the *Rocky* attitude of just wanting to "go the distance" and graduate. I felt a bit overwhelmed by the five different classes I would be attending each week as well as the number of books I was required to read for the semester. Once we started, it took me about six weeks to develop a reading and study schedule that would work around my obligations for my ministry while also allowing time for me to continue my weekly physical exercises. Once I was able to develop a routine and time management schedule, the work began to get easier and less stressful. I very quickly learned that when I was actually interested in the subject matter I was studying, I enjoyed my classes and that the required work was no longer burdensome but enlightening. Those who had applied for the wrong reasons, such as applying just to get a college degree or get away from a facility they did not like, quickly found the work to be a burden and grumbled about coming to class. They became miserable and disdainful toward those who were there for the right reasons and engaging in class discussions. I myself fully believed in the PDP's mission to change the prison culture, and I began to believe that the college education I was getting was in accordance with the will God had for me. I knew that if God brought me to it, he would also see me through it as he had everything else so far. I also knew I was going to have to put in the hard work it was going to take for me

PART II. STORIES OF PERSONAL FAILURE

to finish what I started. Therefore, I set my mind on just following the simple directions that my college director originally told me, which was to just show up for my classes, turn my work in on time, and ask questions.

ACHIEVING BEYOND MY EXPECTATIONS

At the conclusion of my first semester of college, Dr. Perkins called me into his office to pick up my very first transcript, which had my grade point average (GPA) for that semester on it. I received a new sense of confidence when he informed me that I had earned a perfect 4.0 GPA and was one of seven men out of thirty-eight of my fellow PDP students to make the OBU President's Honor Roll! This was a huge personal achievement for me and gave me the motivation to continue putting in the work it took to make those A's. The unexpected news gave me a new confidence that I may actually have what it takes to achieve academic success, which was something I truly thought would be an impossibility just months earlier.

By simply applying myself, following directions, and trusting God, I overcame my fear of failing and greatly exceeded my own expectations by earning a place on the OBU President's Honor Roll with a 4.0 GPA in *both* semesters of my freshman year of college. I even went as far as making both the President's Honor Roll and the Dean's List during the semesters of my sophomore year as well. I have now just completed the final semester of my junior year of college, earning another place on the OBU President's Honor Roll both semesters of my junior year with a 3.89 GPA and am now officially a college senior!

WHAT I HAVE LEARNED ABOUT MYSELF, GOD, AND EDUCATION

What I have learned about myself in the past three years of the Prison Divinity Program is that I am capable of learning at a much higher level than I originally expected. I have also learned that God has placed in me the ability to know him on a deeper level. "We cannot love God deeply without understanding Him fully and we cannot understand Him fully without loving Him deeply."[1] The PPD core curriculum has greatly challenged my knowledge and understanding of God and Scripture and has definitely expanded my thinking in a completely new way. My personal relationship with God has grown by a giant leap as the class lectures, reading assignments, and spiritual journaling have flooded my mind, having a great impact my thinking. The new knowledge that I have gained about God, his world, and my role in it has allowed me to see my prison environment from a new perspective and renewed in me a new passion for education and ministry. I find myself eager to learn what my class instructors have to teach me each new day, and I am ready to put what I learn to work in my prison community, in anticipation of making a difference. Above all, I have learned that God has a much bigger plan for my life in his world than any plan I may have had for myself in it. To accomplish the end goal of that plan, he has provided me the educational resources needed to grow my mind in new ways through the OBU Prison Divinity Program.

THE DIFFERENCE A CHRISTIAN LIBERAL ARTS EDUCATION HAS MADE IN MY LIFE

The "inmate" stamp I currently wear on my back daily may say to the world that I am a failure and have no value or worth in society, but God's word tells me that no matter my past failures and mistakes, I have value and worth and have been uniquely created with intention and purpose. My OBU Christian liberal arts college education has changed my life by connecting me with a larger purpose beyond "self" and has taught me that no matter my past failures, I have value and worth to God and am useable to him, even in a prison. OBU has also taught me that my liberal arts college education is for "the glorification of God."[2] As a Christian

---

1. Perkins, "Nature of Christian Liberal Arts."
2. Fant, *Liberal Arts*, 19.

inmate living in a prison culture, I am aware that God has called me out of darkness to be a light that shines for him in a dark place and that I have an obligation to represent Christ in my prison community in a manner that brings God glory. To bring God glory, I have a responsibility as a disciple of Christ to pursue the type of education that will adequately equip and enable me to share the Bible and teachings of Jesus Christ in a way that those who hear me will be able to see their role in his story of redemption, rescue, and restoration.

CONCLUSION

A fellow mechanic once told me that a mechanic is only as good as the tools he uses. Over the past three years of college, I have learned that God is concerned about my spiritual growth. Through a Christian liberal arts education, he is equipping me with all the necessary tools and resources that I will need to accurately tell his story and live a life worthy of the high calling of God in Christ Jesus. The new knowledge I have gained has given me a life *with* purpose despite having a life without parole sentence. Through my education journey, I have learned that *nothing* is impossible with God, including a college education!

VINCENT TODD OCHOA

Vincent Todd Ochoa is a college student in the Oklahoma Baptist University Prison Divinity Program earning a four-year bachelor's degree in Christian studies at the Lexington Correctional Center in Lexington, Oklahoma. Vince received an ordination for ministry in 2009 from the Friendship Baptist Church of Lawton, Oklahoma. After experiencing a powerful conversion to Christ in 2000, Vince has spent the past twenty-four years of his incarceration facilitating various DOC programs, preaching God's Word, and providing discipleship to new believers, teaching and training men for church leadership. He will graduate college in 2025.

BIBLIOGRAPHY

Perkins, Bruce. "The Nature of Christian Liberal Arts." Cross-Cultural Ministry 1999: Topics in Christian and Cross-Cultural Ministry Studies. Lecture at Oklahoma Baptist University, Lexington, OK, April 29, 2021.

Fant, Gene C., *The Liberal Arts: A Student's Guide*. Wheaton, IL: Crossway, 2012.

PART III

Stories of Personal Perspectives Leading to Embracing Learning

Finding Purpose While Contributing to the Solution

Stages of Growth

Brett Johnson

MY PATH TO EDUCATION

My freedom came to end in 1994 after committing a homicide. Incarceration has been my life since. My outcome was a predictable one. Once, when my uncle came to visit me, he said, "It's no surprise, we all saw this coming." My first arrest was at the age of ten, for arson. This was only the beginning of a wasted life of criminal and destructive behavior. Shoplifting, residential burglary, and auto theft were the usual crimes I committed as a kid. I smoked and used drugs from the age of twelve, which was probably the reason I lashed out in fits of rage at home and never applied myself in school despite having plenty of opportunities and many fresh starts. I continually hurt those around me, and despite repeated attempts by many different authority figures to change the trajectory of my life, I guess I lived up to everyone's expectations, especially mine, seeing as I had none. The attempts by the adults in my life included much patience and love, but I repeatedly wasted every opportunity afforded me.

PART III. STORIES OF PERSONAL PERSPECTIVES

Therapy, probation, counseling, and even one attempt at higher education were just a few of the opportunities I had to change the path I was traveling. When I look back now, I see that one thing each of these have in common is that they require a commitment. However, I knew nothing about setting realistic goals or planning for the long term. My focus was on instant gratification, impressing those around me, and fitting in. I learned at a young age that there were certain people who were impressed by reckless, destructive, and bad behavior. Now that I have the benefit of hindsight, I can see how the people who were impressed by those types of behavior and the behaviors it took to impress them grew riskier and more extreme over time. I felt that, regardless of the consequences, I had to do whatever it took to get a laugh or hear someone say how crazy I was. I cannot believe I ever thought someone calling me crazy would be something I craved or thought helped me fit in. After moving to New Mexico, I attended a different school each year beginning in the fifth grade. I was always the new kid, so it is easy for me to blame this constant state of transition on my desire to fit in and gain approval from my peers, but the truth is I was exhibiting destructive behaviors long before the move to a new state.

CHANGE OF PERSPECTIVE

I brought this type of thinking into prison with me. Even while still in the county jail, my detrimental behavior continued with my fighting officers, breaking windows, and destroying anything I could. I thought this was impressive to those around me, and it was. So, my life, both in and out of prison, was a vicious cycle of getting into trouble, paying the consequences, doing well for a short time, and then getting into trouble again. Anything else would have taken commitment and setting long- and short-term goals for myself, but I saw no value in those things. That word "value" is an important one in this testimony. I did not value commitment and goals; I did not value education; I did not value others; and neither did I value myself. Even though I had my mom, grandparents, aunts, uncles, and all the other adults in my life that cared for and valued me, it wasn't enough. It took God showing me that life is valuable, that even my own wasted life still has value, and that he still has a use for me.

After many years of incarceration, I started working in the prison infirmary. At first, the job consisted of basic janitorial duties; however, I was soon caring for sick and disabled men who could not care for themselves. The road to prison is a familiar one in my world. I recognize in others the need to gain approval and acceptance that drove me for so long, but many of the men I began caring for were not the typical convict. I found myself aiding and assisting veterans, business and legal professionals, doctors, and others who weren't in prison for a systematic lifestyle of bad behavior, but were there for one bad choice or lack of control. I began to realize that even though someone was in prison, there was still value in their life. I began to value other not-so-loveable men, including myself. God had placed me in a position where I could finally learn the life lessons that I had previously failed to learn.

I knew who God was. I had even attended a private Baptist school for a short time. My grandparents were deeply devoted to God and attempted to reveal him to me, but I repeatedly ran from him. I even remember a time when one of my probation officers, out of exasperation, gave me some gospel tracts in a final effort to change the inevitable destination I was trending towards, but my heart was hardened and I was deaf to God's call. Thankfully, he continued to call and pursue me, even when there was no logical reason to. I am likely going to die in prison, and deservedly so, for the things I've done in my life; but praise God, for he uses the people who the world has discarded and who have no value to affect his will and plans. I finally surrendered to his call and he has not failed to deliver on his promises nor show me he is anything but faithful, even when my faith is weak.

PART III. STORIES OF PERSONAL PERSPECTIVES

DESIRE TO SERVE

I began to look for other ways to serve God's kingdom. I still have a heart for ministering in prison infirmaries and even sit with men on their deathbeds, sharing Jesus with them in their final days, but I wanted to do more. I began to feel frustrated with the "revolving door" of the correctional system, a door that I used many times as a juvenile. In one particular case, I knew of a young man who had come to prison six times. For someone who, most likely, will not get another chance at life outside of prison, this is particularly frustrating. I also realize it is equally frustrating for the taxpayers, legislators, and family members of those in here, and, most importantly, for the victims of our crimes and those affected by them. This frustration has motivated me to look for ways to step in where the department of corrections has failed. I can only wonder what the life of that young man who I had seen come and go six times might have looked like if someone started to mentor and disciple him in a different way after the first or second time he came to prison. So, I began to consider being that person, but was ill-equipped for the task. I shared my frustrations with God and he, being the faithful God he is, answered me. Within days, I had his response. While sitting in a cell in a maximum-security prison, I received a memo under my door detailing a new program in which prison inmates would receive a four-year liberal arts degree in Christian studies. Unlike other prison self-improvement programs, this one was open to lifers and men with long sentences. The goal is to change prison culture from within and fill the gaps in the rehabilitation process that the corrections department has not filled. Their vision was the exact vision I had. Oklahoma Baptist University was going to equip me to be the mentor I desired to be.

THE OPPORTUNITY OF A LIFETIME

The Prison Divinity Program came along at the right time in my life. Even a few years sooner and I feel I would have missed this incredible opportunity. God gave OBU the PDP vision at just the right time; a time when I was mentally and spiritually able to make the commitment required of me. Make no mistake, a four-year liberal arts degree at a demanding academic institution like OBU takes commitment. I quickly learned that this was not some watered-down version of college or your typical Department of Corrections program where you only need to show up to graduate. The professors who come into this dark place and teach us men, who many have deemed unteachable, demand excellence. I have learned the importance of setting goals, stewarding my time and available resources, and, most importantly, I have learned critical thinking, which I have lacked my whole life. The PDP has shown me how to use the love and desire to change lives that I hold in my heart to affect people around me, and make a difference that reaches beyond prison walls.

My entire life, people have told me I am highly intelligent, and my grades at OBU reflect this; however, as previously stated, I lacked commitment and never really applied myself to school. My aunt, who has taught at every level of education, tried to teach me its value, but without having a purpose in my life, I never understood the purpose of education. Good grades didn't bring me the instant gratification I desired. I feel the one thing that has changed this is the purpose God has given me. If I want to help change men's lives, if I want to disciple men in how to live a different kind of life, and if I want to show them that there is a different life available to them, I had better apply myself to the things these professors were teaching me. This all-in attitude had unexpected results. I thought I was in the PDP to learn how to change men's lives, but the PDP was transforming my life while, at the same time, teaching me how to be a leader and lead men down a different path.

MY RECIPE FOR SUCCESS

The biggest piece of advice I have for someone considering an education behind bars would be to find out what *your* purpose in life is. There are many programs available in prison. Vocational schools that teach trades have been in prison for years; however, these programs aim to give the short-timer, who will be released in a few years, a means to support himself or, in some cases, a means to support his children and family who are waiting at home. These programs can be effective but fail to address the needs that a transformative education does. There are programs for developing basic living skills, overcoming addiction, and navigating anger management, but often it is overworked case managers who lead them. These individuals only care that you show up for class and have no real way of gauging the success of the program or whether the student is retaining the information in a meaningful, applicable way. The intentions are good, but they fail to address the real needs of the prison inmate. They fail to accomplish a fundamental change in how they think and behave. I feel that a six-month program is inadequate to bring about this complete change of character. So, one must examine himself and find out what they want for their life. In many cases, like mine, following one's purpose must begin with a transformational change within.

Transformational change can only be the result of a deep desire to change and takes time. The second piece of advice I have to offer is to commit to the program. No matter the type of program, for it to be effective, one must fully commit to it and believe it has value for them personally. One thing I have realized is that education is a process. Education is akin to a wall built one brick at a time. Each brick gives the one on top of it a firm foundation and strengthens the entire wall. Many classes and exercises may seem unnecessary, but my experience is that a class I thought held no value as a freshman was now important to me as a junior. Commit to each class and exercise as if your degree depends on it, because it does.

Treat the opportunity to participate in a program like the PDP as the once-in-a-lifetime opportunity that it is. An attitude of gratitude is the most effective way to stay focused and committed to excellence. I remind myself constantly there are many people, law-abiding citizens, who will never have the chance to earn a degree like mine. There is no reason for me to receive this type of favor, but I receive it nonetheless. I thank God for this, and it helps me strive to show my professors and the people generously donating money to the program that I am grateful and appreciative for this chance. It feels like a second chance.

UNEXPECTED FREEDOM

Some might think the phrase "second chance" means the opportunity to get out of prison and have a "do-over." This is not the case with me. Prison is my community, and when I say I feel like I've received a second chance, I mean I now have the opportunity to make a difference in the lives of the people in my world. I know there are mothers and grandmothers out there on their knees praying for someone to pull up their grandsons and tell them about Jesus, for someone to share the gospel with them. I know there are men in here who are tired of doing things their way only for it to end in failure each time. I know these things from my own personal experience. The education I am receiving enables me to be the answer to those prayers and show young men that there is another way to live. Education behind bars is my second chance to live a life with meaning and purpose; I have a second chance to succeed through those whom I will have affected.

I have a gained a sense of freedom the likes of which I have never felt before. I have learned about other cultures and worldviews, as well as how those things have developed and evolved over time. Above all, I have learned how God has revealed himself in history, and used people just like me to further his kingdom and do his will. I know I have value. I know there is still an opportunity to affect others. And, I know this education will continue to have far-reaching impacts on the world in which I live, and even the one in which I do not live. Education has granted me release from prison without stepping foot outside its walls.

PART III. STORIES OF PERSONAL PERSPECTIVES

BRETT JOHNSON

Brett Johnson received a life sentence in 1994. Born in a small town in central Illinois, he moved to Albuquerque, New Mexico, with his mother, younger brother, and older sister. His father was not in the picture, so his mom raised all three kids on her own. She worked hard to support her family and Brett made it harder by getting into trouble often and usually severely. He could blame his troubles on the move from a small farming community to a large city where he was now a minority; however, he was acting out long before then.

For Lack of Knowledge

Jordan Miller

INTRODUCTION

Growing up, I would always get told by my mother that I was "very smart." I admit that learning came easily to me, yet I would sometimes doubt whether I really was smart. I could comprehend work and get it done, no problem; I didn't like it, though, because I felt disconnected from it. I never imagined that education could be the key to open up deeper realms of myself or give me a voice to silence my doubts. As I continued through my first few years of incarceration, I gave my life to Jesus. I declared that I would live for him and dedicate my life to learning and improving who I was. The reason I say "learning" is because God said, "My people are destroyed for a lack of knowledge."[1] I didn't want to be one of those who perished for a lack of not knowing, so I chose to start learning.

I came into the system at a young age. I was a senior in high school one day and an inmate the next. Life can change on a moment's notice and becoming aware of this made me realize that I was on a continual journey. This journey was just beginning and it would be up to me on how I chose to live my life from that

1. Hos 4:6.

point forward. I could go at everything with a negative outlook or I could strive to be better than I ever was or thought I could be. I chose to be like the great men of history—men such as Martin Luther, Justin Martyr, Ignatius of Loyola, Paul, and Jesus—and not let circumstances define me but rather rise above them. However, I was lacking something that they all possessed in their lifetime: an education.

FAILING

Now, the last time I actually went to high school, I had failed. I failed classes left and right. I failed to the point that I needed to go to an alternative academy in order to be on track for graduation. That was just a few months prior to an even greater failure in my life: becoming incarcerated. These were embarrassing moments for a kid who was always told that he was "very smart." I obviously didn't have life figured out. So, needless to say, a higher education seemed scary and foreign to me all these years later, after forgoing school and experiencing multiple failures in my life. The doubts tried to overwhelm me. Can I do this? Am I really smart enough for college? The work, though, how will I do all that stuff? Like the stuff they show in the movies with kids carrying all the books and rushing over research papers. I was panicking, to an extent. What will it be like? Will people understand me? Many questions entered my mind, but the one that I asked myself is "God, is this for me? Can you guide me?" I don't want to perish for a lack of knowledge. So, this transformation started with trusting Jesus before taking my first steps in the right educational direction.

I was fortunate to land at the Lexington Assessment and Reception Center (LARC) when I did. This facility allowed a program called Prison Fellowship Academy to set up a one-year, faith-based program the same year I arrived at this facility. I was very blessed to partake in this program as it was crucial to my growth prior to seeking higher education. This program was the first major step I took in becoming aware that, on this journey, education was bigger than just being knowledgeable in any one area. It became a part of who I was. It became my responsibility to become educated. This led me to a deeper interest in wanting to learn. I started to seek out higher education opportunities and any transformative learning programs that the facility had to offer.

I soon saw that education is the key that unlocks the door to a brighter future. It is a powerful tool that empowers individuals and transforms societies. For me, embracing education is not just about acquiring knowledge but is about nurturing curiosity, fostering critical thinking, and developing essential skills that enable us as individuals to thrive. We live in an ever-changing world. If I am not educated on the fact that education itself is a tool or how to survive the changes, I am doomed to fail. Every aspect of life requires a sense of knowledge. How could I be wise like Jesus if I wasn't learned? I soon got the opportunity to become learned when Oklahoma Baptist University and the department of correction was moved by God to bring education into the prison system. Higher education has helped me to understand that being educated is truly a lifelong journey that begins the moment we are born. It starts with the nurturing care and guidance provided by our parents and caregivers. It continues through formal schooling, higher education, and beyond. I see life as a continuous process of learning, unlearning, and relearning. It never ends. So becoming educated by a Christian liberal arts university that equips individuals like me with the knowledge, skills, and attitudes necessary to navigate the complexities of life was a pure blessing to me. I now see the benefits of the acquisition of knowledge, embracing learning, and helping others grow along the way.

SO WHAT? BENEFITS OF EMBRACING EDUCATION

One of the primary benefits I have experienced by embracing education is the acquisition of knowledge. I love how education broadens my worldview, exposes me to new ideas, and helps me make sense of the world around me. It also provides me with a deeper understanding of various subjects, ranging from math and science to literature and history. Knowledge is not just about facts, though. I see it as a powerful tool that enables me to make informed decisions, solve problems, and contribute meaningfully to society. Such knowledge is a tool that I previously undervalued and took for granted. Another thing this transformative education has done for me is foster critical thinking and analytical skills. It encourages you to question, evaluate, and challenge existing ideas and beliefs. By developing critical thinking skills and integrating faith, I am becoming better equipped to analyze complex issues, make sound judgments, and arrive at well-reasoned conclusions. This ability to think critically is essential in today's society, where information and misinformation are equally accessible and things happen in the blink of an eye. Embracing higher education empowers us to distinguish between fact and fiction, enabling us to make informed choices and navigate the hardships of today's age.

In addition to knowledge and critical thinking, education also equips me with essential life skills. These skills include communication, problem-solving, teamwork, adaptability, and resilience. Higher education provided me with opportunities to develop these skills through various activities such as group projects, presentations, and extracurricular activities. These skills are not only crucial for personal success but also for thriving in the workplace and contributing to the development of society. I hope you're following the progression at this point. Embracing education is a big deal! It has impacted every aspect of life for me. Through this transformative education, doors open to opportunities that would otherwise be inaccessible to those incarcerated like myself. If you give it a chance it will empower you to overcome obstacles, break free from the cycle of poverty and addiction, and create a better future for yourself and your family. For me, it instilled feelings of confidence, self-worth, and independence that are as irreplaceable as my faith in Jesus. This experience enables us to take control of our lives in a healthy manner and make a positive impact on the world.

When it comes to moral rehabilitation, embracing education has had a profound impact on my personal growth and self-empowerment. People need to know they are better than the sin they committed as well as the nature of sin they were residing in, just like I needed to know. Faith-integrated programs are necessary to get to the heart of the matters going on inside of men and women across facilities nationwide. They are great for rehabilitation as they get you to focus on your responsibility for your actions, thoughts, and mishaps. No more hiding from the person in the mirror. More than that, the best thing these programs get you to understand is that you never had things figured out in life, you were never in control, you weren't doing anything on your own power, and you were never alone, because Jesus was there all along just waiting for you to return to him. Having good morals is something that you may have to be educated on as well. Through integrative faith education, they actually get you to start adopting the mind(set) of Christ, aligning with him in thought and deed.

In the divided world we live in today, higher education is needed to also promote social mobility, reduce inequality, and foster social cohesion by providing equal opportunities for success to individuals from diverse backgrounds. Higher education empowers men like me to challenge social norms, advocate for change, and cultivate the belief that I can contribute to the betterment of society. Embracing education is not just an individual endeavor; it is a collective responsibility that requires the commitment and support of governments, communities, and stakeholders. For the incarcerated individuals, this support must come from our staff members and peers. It is crucial to have one, unified vision and support system in order to embrace higher learning. This brings to mind the phrase "teamwork makes the dream work."

In conclusion, embracing education is essential for personal growth, societal development, and economic progress. Education empowers individuals with the knowledge, critical thinking skills, and essential life skills necessary to thrive in an ever-changing world. It opens doors to opportunities, fosters personal growth, and enables individuals to make a positive impact on society. Education is changing the lives of men around me daily. It's something to smile about when you see growth/change happen in someone else's life. Each day, I get to study the life of the

Savior of the world and learn about the history that comes with it—an opportunity I would have never had without integrated faith learning. I feel so honored and privileged at the fact that I get to be a part of it; it is a humbling experience. I didn't seek out an education to become a know-it-all or fancy pants; I sought it out because I knew that my Lord and Savior, Jesus, didn't want me to perish for a lack of knowledge. He wanted me to know him and know myself, to love him and love myself, and to share him with others. The only way I could do these things was by embracing education. I embraced this transformative learning experience because Jesus embraced me.

5 STRATEGIES/SUGGESTIONS TO EMBRACE LEARNING

1. Trust Jesus. In order to do anything in life and be truly successful, you must trust in Jesus and the plans he has in store for you. At one point in my life, during my incarceration, I thought I would never do another school-related thing. God had other plans. My mom used to tell me, "Son, don't quench the spirit." If you feel that a higher education experience or transformative learning opportunity is what is needed in your facility, home, or life, I suggest that you trust Jesus and don't quench the spirit, brother or sister.

2. Believe in yourself. I must put this disclaimer in here: you will fail, but that is okay. Have enough faith in yourself to not quit after the first mistake. You can still achieve great things when you just believe that you can do it. Don't let self-doubt creep up on you. Remember that you can do all things in Christ who strengthens you.

3. Embrace the entire learning experience. Do not cheat yourself out of the opportunity to grow in this experience. Don't give halfhearted attempts, or your growth will reflect it. As the saying goes, "You'll get out of it what you put into it." Don't let anything hold you back from reaching the potential that you

could reach. Treat yourself by showing up each day ready to get to work and being grateful for the opportunity that God has blessed you with, even in the current circumstance. Embrace the highs and lows but never get stuck there.

4. Challenge yourself (get out of your comfort zone). One of my favorite quotes comes from John Maxwell, who says, "Be a thermostat, not a thermometer."[2] I love this quote because it fits perfectly for prison: you can either make change happen in this place or you get changed by this place. You cannot sit in places of familiarity and expect to grow. You must be the change agent for your environment. Part of the embracing learning part is that you get out of what makes you comfortable to learn new things. How else does one expand their horizons in life? Be ready to accept the new, daunting task of higher education. It was scary to me too, at first, and I'm the guy who said learning was easy and natural for me. But I believe in you, just as Jesus and countless others have believed in me.

5. Have a source of motivation. Make sure you have a continual source for motivation. For me, I have Jesus (of course), my daughter Jayla'Nae, my fiancé, my parents, and my siblings. I draw motivation from these sources daily. They still see me for who I really am and not the mistake I made, which makes me strive even harder to make them proud.

JORDAN MILLER

Glory be to God. Jordan Miller is honored at the opportunity to share a piece of his journey with you all. Jordan prays that this chapter encourages someone to see education in a new light and that it also reaches hardened hearts. We are all on a journey and he implores you to take advantage of opportunities for growth and do not be afraid to believe in yourself. He is looking forward

---

2. Maxwell, *Maxwell Daily Reader*, 96.

to continuing his educational journey and returning home to his family and community. He wants to thank everyone who has invested in his journey of education. Peace be with you, Amen.

BIBLIOGRAPHY

Christian Standard Bible. Nashville, TN: Holman Bible, 2018.
Maxwell, John C. *The Maxwell Daily Reader.* Nashville: Thomas Nelson, 2007.

Not Perfect Yet Useable

Roscoe LaRett Morris

SUDDENLY, WITH JUST A few minutes left in my second-grade elementary class on November 22, 1963, there came an emergency announcement over the school intercom system. John F. Kennedy had been assassinated. Fear struck the classroom full of seven-year-old children. The news devastated the children and adults alike. Administrators immediately dismissed school for the remainder of the day. Just imagine for a second, a room full of seven-year-old children. Can you see their confused and frightened faces as they were rushed from their classroom and told to go home? As one of those wide-eyed little boys, I thought the world was ending.

Six years later, on April 4, 1968, my mother, three older siblings, and I were visiting my Aunt Louis. During the peaceful quiet of another normal day, it happened again. Breaking news reports on the radio and television informed us that Dr. Martin Luther King, Jr. had just been shot and killed.

Both President Kennedy and Dr. King were well known catalysts for change in American society. They were united in the fight against racism. Both of these great men were against violence as a means for social change. These two tragic, unforgettable moments in history inspired me and left me with a lifelong desire to seek an education. Contemplating their sacrifices brings to mind an even more profound act of selflessness; Jesus Christ laid his life down so that mankind could live together in fellowship with God. My own life has been saved by Jesus. He is the reason I am here to share my story with you.

Coinciding with the tragic events of that time, addiction and dysfunction relentlessly corrupted the fabric of my family. Mom and Dad were dedicated parents, but they were having their difficulties. Dad worked all week to provide for us, yet he was plagued by alcohol addiction. That addiction led to many predictable dysfunctions in our family. My childhood experiences were beset with moments of fear and uncertainty due to the erratic conditions present within my home. Nevertheless, throughout my entire life I have held firmly to my belief in the importance of education.

Throughout my junior high school days, I was forced to fend for myself. My family had moved into an all-white neighborhood. This was somewhat of a culture shock to me. Though most of my dad's friends were white, the whites in this new neighborhood did not seem to want to adjust to the idea of having blacks around them. Making things even harder, the Tulsa Public School system integrated during my second year in junior high school. I recall going home many days in tears. The new black kids in the school teased me because they thought that I talked like a white. The white parents felt put upon and angry that their children were forced to go to school with blacks. The racial tension forced upon all of us had become so thick that you could cut it with a butter knife. We were all just kids; I don't believe any of us understood why our skin color was such a big issue in society.

It was during my ninth-grade year of junior high that I found out that my mother had not completed high school. Seeing how she struggled and realizing how her lack of education affected her life further fueled my desire for an education. I realized later that I had a mistaken motive for completing school. I thought that finishing high school was primarily for the satisfaction of my parents. My thoughts about my own education were so tied up with my thoughts about my parents that the desire for my mother to complete high school with me caused me to beg her to join me in school and graduate with me.

I felt it would be spectacular having my mother in school with me. However, she believed the devil's lie that I would be embarrassed having her there. Looking back, perhaps having Mom there would have led me to be more attentive to my academic studies, but Mom didn't join me.

I believe it was at this time that my own worldview was overtaken by society's attitudes toward me, and it was at this time that the ways of the world began taking a strong hold on my behaviors. My older siblings were getting married and starting their own families. As the youngest child, this had a great effect on me. I no longer had a big sister or big brothers looking out for me. This put me in a position at a critical age where I was on my own to search for what my life really meant. I remember well my adolescent thoughts at the time. Who was I? Where was my place in this journey of life?

I had watched my dad for years. He was an excellent provider for the family, yet he lived what I considered to be a dull life, dominated by his struggle with alcohol addiction. I told myself I would never follow that road.

The world had other ideas. I was a teenager and, at this stage of life, all the kids I was hanging around were smoking marijuana. Very foolishly, I decided to try marijuana. Shortly after that first inhalation I found myself addicted. Marijuana oppressed my life just like alcohol had done to my dad. When Mom discovered which road I was traveling, she sat me down and warned me how marijuana was a gateway drug that would lead me to addiction to other more dangerous drugs, but I did not heed her warning.

By the time I graduated from high school, my life had spun out of control just as my mother had predicted. This caused chaos for society and for myself. The marijuana addiction had led me to crack cocaine. Crack was the drug Mom had been most frightened of. This drug took such hold on me that I became completely lost. Under the influence of crack, I made horrible decisions that caused me to lose four wives, my relationship with my son, and any hope of a relationship with his children. Even though Mama never had anything to do with drugs, she surely knew what they would do to me.

A big change came when, through the saving power of Jesus Christ, I got clean. Coming to my senses was painful. I found myself in prison on a long fourth stint. This is when the word *education* came rushing back, over and over, into my mind. I felt a sense of responsibility to finally get an education that would allow me to contribute to the betterment of society.

Prison is tough. Each day there are obstacles thrown my way. Those obstacles attempt to pull me away from the pursuit of learning. Nevertheless, when things seem to be more than I can handle, I recall the great sacrifices that have been made so that I can have this chance to complete my sentence and, at the same time, get an education. Because of the people who followed Jesus' example of self-sacrifice—people like John Kennedy and Martin Luther King Jr.—I have this chance, and I intend to see it through so that when my chance comes to re-enter society outside these walls, I will be equipped to join the ranks of those who use their education to put the well-being of others ahead of their own.

At this point it would be reasonable for the reader to wonder, "Why would someone go through several prison terms and finally come to his senses?" Well, there comes a time in life when one like me, who is under the spell of addiction, hits rock bottom. That is a cliché people have used for years, but it is also an unavoidable truth. A time comes when you come face-to-face with yourself in the mirror, and peering into that mirror, you cannot deny the need for a transformative action on your own part. I came to that point in my life. I was stuck and in pain, and I knew I could not continue in the direction I was headed. That is when it really became clear that there was profound truth in what the heroes of my life had told me about an education. I had become certain that without an education, there would be no forward movement toward my purpose on this earth.

Thanks be to God for stirring the hearts of people with authority to begin a liberal arts school of academic studies for people in prison. Oklahoma Baptist University started up the Prison Divinity Program and my prayers had been answered. Our ever-faithful God once again provided the opportunity for me to get an education. All the voices from my past came rushing forth, encouraging me to learn. My decision to apply to OBU was an easy one, and I could see my mother smiling as I filled out the paperwork. There have been several challenges along the way on this academic adventure. I was not fully prepared academically to launch right into the challenging curriculum of a prestigious Christian liberal arts university like OBU, but I am completely determined to see it through. I will confide that there have been some confidence-shattering moments, but as they say, where there is no pain there can be no gain. Each day brings about the challenge of discouragement, but I remind myself of what I have come through and that this education will allow me to flourish while helping others in society.

I remember Dad telling me a story about how to overlook what people say about you. There were so many times I recall going home from school crying because of what someone had said about my mother or about me. The first thing Dad would say to me was, "Do they know anything about you or your mother?" My reply never failed to bring a smile to my face, because surely the answer was, "No, Dad. They don't." In the same way, most of the people who may be talking about me now know nothing about me. With that knowledge, there is nothing that can make me doubt my ability to learn and teach others what I am learning.

Reflecting back on everything that has transpired in my life fuels my desire for learning. As challenges seem to surge, so does my drive for learning and teaching others what I have learned. Liberal arts studies have given a wide understanding of Western culture as well as my role as a Christian working within it to change it for the better. Before I learned about liberal arts studies, I thought that you had to have a specific technical field of study before even going to college. Now that I have been involved with OBU's liberal arts program, I know how important it is for one to have a broad, perspective-building education. Studying classical literature and Western civilization has given me a perspective on how the world has come to be the way it is. This knowledge is invaluable. I understand my place in history as part of the postmodern age.

This liberal arts program that I am so blessed to be a part of has given me the desire for looking not at what a man is but what is possible in him. My perspective of life has taken on a completely new outlook on not only my destination but also the destination of all humankind. One major problem with the world today is that everybody seems to be concerned with himself or herself. Too few people think about what he or she can do for others. The liberal arts program opened my eyes to how and why learning is vital for life. How do you tell a man how to make pancakes if you have never made them yourself? Therefore, for me to be of any use in society, I must have something to offer.

There had to be a change in my life. Without education, my life was shaping up to be a waste of time and space. I truly believe that without this education, there would be little hope for me nor for my ability to lead anyone toward a better life direction. This education will allow me to work while I am in prison as well as after I get out, working with those people who are at-risk and in need. This pursuit will allow me to contribute toward my heart's desire for there to be a decrease in incarceration not only in this state but also throughout the world.

I am far from perfect, yet right now, I am a senior in good standing with the Prison Divinity Program. Today I know that my thirst for education is being satisfied in a way that will make me useful to my family, to my church, and to society.

STRATEGIES AND SUGGESTIONS

Here are a few strategies and suggestions for changing the culture of the prison system. Education in the form of structured degree programs should be at the top of the list. Exposure to the word of God is also critical, but most convicted people have heard someone preach to them. Preaching has its place and time. However, once someone has heard the message, it becomes necessary to take action. Action requires application. Application allows the listeners to be involved and feel as if they have a part in whatever we are trying to accomplish. Every institution faces its own challenges, but in order to effect positive change, those who are to be changed must be actively involved in the mission of the institution. Inmates will respond if they are recognized as stakeholders. After all, the vast majority of inmates will be released from prison. Someday, these inmates will be in line with everyone else at the grocery store. Inmates that got out last week are there now. Treating these inmates as valuable assets and stakeholders during their incarcerations will change the way they behave when they get to the checkout counter.

Many good messages are spoken to inmates, but only when you allow the listeners to become involved is there a commitment, and that commitment brings about the change you are seeking to achieve. With commitment comes ownership. Everyone wants to preach and assign ownership, but the fact is that inmates are not being prepared and equipped to take on the responsibility of that ownership.

When education becomes the prime mission of the institutions of incarceration, there will be less and less need for prisons. The majority of prisoners have never learned the difference between a problem and a solution. Incarceration will evolve eventually into a primarily educational system. Until then, inmates will continue to come out of prison without the perspective and problem-solving skills needed by society.

ROSCOE LARETT MORRIS

Roscoe LaRett Morris was born to Billy Mack and Barbara Jean Morris in Tulsa, Oklahoma. He is the youngest of four children. His educational background from K–12 was through the Tulsa Public School System. From his youth, his dad and his dad's oldest sister (Aunt Louis) instilled within him a yearning for education. Aunt Louis always encouraged him with these words: "Roscoe, you can achieve whatever you set your mind to accomplish." His dad always told him, "Son, an education is the one thing no man can take from you."

From Death to Life

Christopher Whinery

MY EDUCATIONAL EXPERIENCE STARTED at a young age. I am the youngest of five, raised by my father and stepmother. Naturally, by the time I was reaching school age, there were many educational materials to be found around the house, thanks to my siblings. Before I started school, my stepmom began teaching me the alphabet, among other things. I recall a memory of getting frustrated, but Mom was relentless. She would allow me to step away for a few moments, only to have me return and accomplish the task.

I guess you could say she is the reason for my early love of education. As I got older, I strove to learn. Other kids my age were playing outside during the summer, riding bikes and rollerblading. Although I also engaged in these activities, I enjoyed playing school. I would ask one of my siblings to be the teacher and to give me homework using one of their workbooks from previous classes. Everything that was put before me was a challenge that I wanted to defeat.

That zeal for education never left me. In the third grade, I won my class spelling bee. This allowed me to compete at the school spelling bee for grades three to five. I finished as runner-up. When I misspelled my word and had to leave the stage, I cried. I wanted to do better. I realize now that this was a major accomplishment for a third grader and not something to be ashamed of.

While in the seventh grade, I joined the math and science club. Meetings were every other Saturday morning at the school. While other children were eating their cereal in front of their Saturday morning cartoons, I was participating in quiz bowls and dissecting owl pellets. I thoroughly enjoyed doing these things.

The tenth grade was the one and only time I have ever failed a class. I found some new excitement in my life that was beginning to take the place of education . . . girls. I was in an English class with my girlfriend at the time. Instead of paying attention in class and excelling on my quizzes, I was busy passing notes. When those report cards came out, I was devastated. I knew my parents were going to be disappointed, and I was ashamed.

After experiencing this failure, I realized I needed to balance my personal life and academics. I did not give up pursuing girls, but I also did not let my grades slip again. Actually, I began to push myself harder. In the eleventh grade, I was at the top of my math class and realized that I was becoming bored with it. After speaking with my math teacher, I was enrolled in an advanced placement (AP) algebra course. Little did I know, "AP" just means lots of homework. It was a challenge for me, and I loved it!

One month into my junior year, our country experienced tremendous tragedy. On September 11, 2001, while sitting in my math class, I watched on television as two planes hit the World Trade Center. Something was stirred within me, and I knew from that moment that I wanted to do something about it. At the age of seventeen, with parental consent, I joined the United States Air Force and entered the Delayed Entry Program. I would be leaving for basic training after the completion of my senior year.

Looking back, I wish I had pushed myself sooner. Having good grades and only one AP course did not make me a likely candidate for college scholarships. I guess not applying for said scholarships did not help any either. Coming from a family of five, I honestly did not see college in my future. Plus, by this time, I had already resolved to enlist in the military.

I am extremely proud to be a fourth-generation veteran. My great-grandfather, grandfather, and father all served in the United States Army. Needing parental consent, I first approached my father about joining the Marine Corps. However, late 2001 and early 2002 saw a huge increase in military casualties. Not wanting to receive the news of his youngest son being killed in action, my father refused to sign. After much debate, my father finally agreed to sign the papers for me to join the Air Force instead. The plan was to enlist for computer networking; however, upon leaving the Military Enlistment Processing Station, I had joined as "open-mechanical." This meant that I would be placed into any mechanical position.

On February 17, 2004, I enlisted into the Air Force as an Aircraft Armament Systems Specialist. Essentially, I was a bomb loader (also referred to as a "load toad"). With my enlistment into the Air Force, I thought my academic years were behind me. I quickly learned that was not the case. Between basic training, technical school, and on-the-job training, I was constantly in class and taking tests. However, just as in high school, I excelled in a classroom environment and at test taking.

On Mother's Day 2005, I deployed to Bagram Air Base in Afghanistan. It was here that I started my journey toward earning my first degree. Even though I was working twelve-hour days, I had plenty of free time on my hands. A co-worker and I went to the education office on base and inquired about College Level Examination of Proficiency (CLEP) tests. I took my first CLEP in June 2005, giving me my first three credits towards my associate degree from the Community College of the Air Force. I returned home in September 2005 and immediately reported to the education office to sign up for classes. Over the next two years, I took two classes: Statistics from Campbell University and United States History from Central Texas College. The overall goal was to complete my associate before discharging from the Air Force. Unfortunately, a back injury in September 2005 led to an early discharge and prevented me from completing my degree with that college.

After four years in the Air Force, I suddenly found myself without a job. I felt as if I had lost my identity. I entered the civilian workforce and quickly realized the need to continue my education. Unloading trucks at Walmart was not what I had planned for my life. I enrolled into my first classes at University of Phoenix in the fall of 2010. During my online orientation course, I realized online classes were not for me. Who knew you could fail an orientation course? Fortunately, the university also provided ground classes at a local campus in Wichita, Kansas, where I was living. I was able to take classes while still maintaining a full-time job. This worked perfectly for me.

There were a few setbacks along the way, but I completed my bachelor's in criminal justice administration in February 2014. At the time of my graduation, I was working as a night custodian for Sapulpa High School. Upon completion of my degree, I put in an application at a state agency to begin my career in criminal justice. However, as circumstance would have it, this career was short lived.

In January 2015, I was charged with first-degree murder and placed in county jail. Nine months later, the state successfully filed the Bill of Particulars in my case. That meant that if I were convicted, the state would seek to take my life by lethal injection. I felt defeated; life for me was over.

As a young boy, I was always interested in church. I would ride my bike to church as many as three times a week. It felt like home to me. I learned about Christ and his salvation. I was baptized at a young age, but to be honest, I did it because all my friends were doing it. I did not understand the true meaning of baptism. One of two things happen to people in county jail: they get fit or find Jesus. I did both. I lost seventy pounds and came back into fellowship with my Savior. My relationship with Christ at this time was paramount to me making it through this experience.

Over the next few years, life for me had become routine. Wake up, eat, read, watch television, sleep. The cycle became monotonous. I felt as if I had no purpose and was ready to succumb to just being another number. However, this was not the plan God had for me.

I spent much of 2020 on COVID lockdown and realized there was something missing in my life. After calling out to God for a change, I saw a flier for the Prison Divinity Program through Oklahoma Baptist University. My first reaction was "Absolutely not." I had already received a degree. Was I ready to put in that kind of work again? God answered for me, "Absolutely." My criminal justice administration degree had turned into nothing more than a piece of paper the moment I became a convicted felon. What would a felon do with that kind of degree? God was giving me an opportunity to get an education in something I could use. However, I still had to fill out an application and be accepted. I felt as if it was a long shot.

I am currently in the spring semester of my junior year and am maintaining a 4.0 grade point average. I realize that when I am in the pursuit of knowledge, I am at my best. I found my purpose in life again. Not only am I getting an education in Christian studies, but also God has given me the ability to help others in the process. As stated previously, I love math. In the fall semester of 2022, we started a course in contemporary mathematics. It involved everything from inductive and deductive reasoning to geometry, algebra, and finance. I was in my element. This gave me the opportunity to help other men who were struggling with this course. Out of thirty-eight men, thirty-six passed the course. I began to realize a calling God had on my life: teaching.

Teaching is not limited to the classroom. It can also be performed in the church. I would have never guessed I would ever preach the gospel. However, I delivered my first sermon on July 15, 2022. My education with OBU has given me the ability to correctly exegete Scripture, and accurately deliver God's word to the world. We have been told repeatedly that Scripture is for transformation not just information. I believe the same could be said about my education experience through OBU. It gives men the power to transform the lives of those around them. This transformation does not stop at the fence; it extends into the world outside of the confines of prison.

I have been fortunate enough to experience education through a secular university as well as a Christian liberal arts university. In both of them, I received knowledge. However, a Christian liberal arts degree differs in that I am not just receiving knowledge but am also experiencing a life-altering transformation. A Christian liberal arts education makes you think critically. It has developed an ability to wrestle with the hard questions and understand God's world. I am receiving knowledge and deepening my walk with Christ at the same time. It also allows me to encourage others to do the same.

I should never have been given the opportunity to enroll into the Prison Divinity Program. The extent of my prison sentence was supposed to be to spend the rest of my life on death row . . . but God delivered me from that death sentence. I was instead sentenced to life with the possibility of parole. God intervened in my life and gave me the opportunity to pursue a transformational education and extend that experience to others. I have literally gone from death to life—a life of opportunity and speaking life into others.

The Oklahoma Department of Corrections has a new slogan, "We Change Lives."[1] While I hope this proves to be true, I believe that with the assistance of the men of God—as I have experienced through the PDP and OBU—lives will truly be changed. Transformative education does not always take place in a classroom; sometimes it takes place through a tray slot, a locked door, in a chapel, or in a prison dorm. There is no obstacle too great when we are doing God's work.

One of my life verses is Philippians 2:3, which states, "Do nothing out of selfish ambition or conceit, but in humility consider others as more important than yourselves."[2] Paul uses the Greek word ὑπερέχοντας (pronounced "hyperechontas"), which means to considering others as more valuable. In this sense, transformative learning is putting the needs of others above your own. We have seen this repeatedly with our director, Dr. Bruce Perkins, as well as with various professors who have given their time to come teach some men who have been considered castaways. This education

1. Flemming, "Offender Advocacy," para. 1.
2. Phil 2:3.

has given men their purpose back; it has restored relationships and brought hundreds to Christ.

STRATEGY SUGGESTIONS

I believe embracing learning has shaped who I am as a man today. I know I have not always made all the right decisions, but my educational journey has had a tremendous impact on my life and character. In order to embrace learning you must realize that you have worth and potential. Dig deep and practice some personal reflection to see the worth and potential for your own lives. Educators who are considering this style of teaching must have an ὑπερέχοντας mindset. Make sure your students feel valued and that their needs are being met; when students feel as if they matter, they will push themselves. It is imperative that incarcerated students are not treated any differently. I am grateful that we are not receiving a watered-down education, but the same education given on the Shawnee campus. However, if your students are asking for assistance in understanding the materials, be sure to help them in any way possible.

My best advice on embracing learning is to make it your life goal. I have made learning and education priorities in my life. I have realized that my life had more meaning and purpose when I am in pursuit of knowledge. Again, this does not always have to mean academic. Your pursuit of knowledge could be biblical or relational. Under no circumstances should you give up the pursuit of knowledge.

CHRISTOPHER WHINERY

Christopher Whinery is the youngest of five in a blended family and is a veteran of the United States Air Force. Going to church was not a priority in his household. However, around the age of twelve or thirteen, he started going to church on his own, often riding his bike the six blocks to church. As a young adult, he did not have a relationship with God. After he was medically discharged from the military, God started moving in him. Upon his arrest, Christopher questioned God's presence. Looking back, he can see that God never left him.

BIBLIOGRAPHY

Christian Standard Bible. Nashville: Holman Bible, 2018.
Flemming, Nicole. "Offender Advocacy." About, Oklahoma Department of Corrections. https://oklahoma.gov/doc/about/offender-advocacy.html.

The Christian Liberal Arts
Educating All on the Momentum Inherent in Christian Redemption, Rehabilitation, and Restoration

James Joseph Wymer Jr.

AN OKLAHOMA EDUCATION

IN ORDER TO PROPERLY convey to you, dear reader, my personal perspective on experiencing life transformation through Jesus Christ and receiving a Christian liberal arts education, more than a little context may be necessary. So, as I weave my tale, bear in mind that the life experiences we have at and during our school years, as well as throughout everyday life, profoundly shape who and what we become. If, like me, as you will soon read, you have experienced trauma at school, get help *now*. Please do not wait. While it is never too late to get help, the story I am about to share with you happened when I was thirteen to fifteen years old, but I did not become aware of the weight those events had placed on my soul until I was forty-six years old. I could have lived the rest of my life walking around not knowing what was creating the bitterness in my heart and killing me with hate, but God had other plans—plans to heal, to make whole, and to further transform my life with a Christian liberal arts education. While God is not confined to any preconceived human notions of his working, it was during the process of my engaging with this rigorous curriculum where revelation and insight into my long festering wounds from thirty years ago were given to me and the process of healing began. It is my reckoning that, inherent within my story, you will find gems that may bring about personal insight into the definitive role that our experiences derived from the giving and receiving of an education bear in the whole of our lives. Please, let us begin.

I was born the only child of two sixteen-year-olds and was raised for the better part by my grandparents and my mom. Neither of my parents finished high school. I began my school career when I was enrolled in kindergarten at Jefferson Davis Elementary in southeast Oklahoma City in 1981. I was only four years old at the time of enrollment, as I would not turn five until August 19, which would be right after school officially started. Because of this, the staff tried to persuade my mom to wait a year to enroll me. However, she simply grabbed a book off the desk and asked me to read it. I was able to do so because I loved to read, write, and do my numbers. Once the school staff realized this, they tried to persuade my mom to enroll me in the second grade. My mom declined and, alas, she would decline every time school officials would ask to move me forward two or three grades, which happened throughout my school years until I reached the ninth grade.

Jumping ahead to 1990, while I was at Thomas Jefferson Middle School, eighth graders across Oklahoma were taking the PSAT. The following year, officials used the results of that test to offer those with the highest scores an opportunity to enroll in the Oklahoma School of Science and Mathematics. I was offered one of those opportunities. Unfortunately, I declined the opportunity without proper counsel, as any counsel I might have had regarding the enormity of the possibilities innate in such an opportunity was neither offered nor sought. By my own counsel, I thought I was a future football hero and did not want to mess that up by going to a school that did not have a football team. Obviously, this is one of those moments in life when you look back and wonder, "What if I had sought out or been given wise counsel in that moment?" Even so, I had no inkling then, or for awhile yet, that God had his own plans for my gaining a transformative education.

To that end, God's plan involved my experiencing life in such a way that I developed a unique perspective on both the education system and the justice system in Oklahoma. Case in point: the same year I took the PSAT at Jefferson Middle School, a classmate, Lamont "Huggie" Fields, would bring a handgun to school and shoot his former friend and classmate, Tito Carter, three times. Tito would live and go on to North West Classen High School. Meanwhile, Lamont would go on to have a very profound effect on Oklahoma and its justice system in 1996 when he walked away from a department of corrections work center in Oklahoma City and killed his girlfriend and her parents. After his unfathomable crime, Lamont was shot and killed by police. Such a horrible, tragic, and senseless loss of life coming on the heels of the even more horrible, tragic, and senseless bombing of the Murray building the year before was more than enough reason for inflammatory tough-on-crime rhetoric and ensuing tough-on-crime policies to be implemented in Oklahoma (e.g., the support of private prisons, the removal of the Pell Grant, and the enactment of the 85 percent statute with inequitable sentencing). The bitter and fearful rhetoric as well as the resulting dehumanizing corrections policies skewed Oklahoma's justice system from being an opportunity for rehabilitation, education, growth, and eventual reconciliation, to becoming a systemic warehouse of dehumanization with no recourse for hope, repentance, healing, or reconciliation. It is easy to justify rhetoric and actions such as these in a society that is already prepared to strip some human beings of their humanity when those humans break society's laws. But the truth is and always will be that lawbreakers are still human beings.

During my sophomore year at Capitol Hill High School, when I was fifteen years old, I moved in with a friend and had to transfer to Douglass High School. On February 8, 1992, of that same school year, my friend, Charles "Billy" Graham, was shot in the head while he was standing at his locker. At the time of Billy's shooting, I was out by his car waiting for him when some other friends came running out of the school yelling at me that someone shot Billy. I took off running inside and up the stairs and found him lying in front of his locker, surrounded by onlookers, with another friend holding his head. I started asking what happened and was told that Billy's girlfriend's ex-boyfriend had walked up behind Billy and shot him. Billy did not die immediately as a result of the shooting and, following this event, was in a vegetative state with only a ventilator keeping him breathing. After conferring with doctors who did not want to perform surgery to go in after the bullet lodged in Billy's brain, for fear of doing more damage than good, Billy's mom would make the heart-crushing decision to turn off his ventilator. We (his friends) were given the opportunity to go in and say goodbye to Billy before she did. After Billy's funeral, I dropped out of school and become a full-time addict and thief. By December 15, 1992, less than a year after Billy's death, I was in the Oklahoma County jail facing fourteen felony charges on seven separate cases. It seems poignant to me now when I see on the news how counselors are provided for students who go through what I went through, as it seems society now has a more compassionate understanding of the trauma innate in such events and of the deep need to alleviate that trauma and allow it to breathe and heal.

During the time I spent in the county jail, I came to Christ again (I was previously saved at six years old and baptized at ten years old). Daily, I started immersing myself in his word through prayer and studying Scripture. After ten months in the Oklahoma County Jail, I was sent to the Lexington Assessment and Reception Center and, by extension, into the Oklahoma Department of Corrections with a twenty-year prison sentence. I was seventeen years old. At this time, I believed that God instilled in me the imperative importance of education, so I hit the ground running and quickly earned my GED. I was then led to inquire about college and took the ACT. Surprising to some, I scored well on my ACT and was soon enrolled in college. While my grades at that time reflected my tendency for procrastination more than any lack of ability, I was able to remain on the right path and enjoy the process. At this time, I was blessed to have a positive influence in the coordinator of the college program, Mr. Ted Roberts, who was a viable and constant source of encouragement for me and the other men in the college program. Mr. Roberts, a lifelong educator, had found a second career in facilitating the pursuit of a college education by the incarcerated. He was an avid supporter of the college program, of us, and of the way in which we were renewing our minds, but did not tolerate much foolishness. However, I would soon lose my only means of affording college when Pell Grants were stripped from all prisoners across the nation. Left to my own devices, I all too soon strayed from my education as well as the way of the Lord, as I progressively bought into the lie of prison culture and joined a prison gang. As a result, I served ten and a half years of that twenty-year sentence and was released April 4, 2003, without a single tangible job skill gained during my stay in prison. Maybe this particular episode should be seen and remembered as both an example of an educator and a student with the heart, head, and hands necessary to cultivate positive life transformation in others and themselves, while also being a cautionary tale against the implementation of impediments that strip educators and students of their abilities and their opportunities, irrespective of where they are.

Having completed my prison sentence regardless of my state of readiness to enter polite society again, enter it I did, confident that I could handle anything and everything. Unfortunately, I all too soon mishandled the whole thing, as the false persona I had assumed for myself during my time in prison found me on my way back to prison after just twenty-six months of freedom. I was arrested and charged with first-degree burglary when I broke into the home of a drug dealer who had stolen two hundred dollars from me. In turn, I stole his television set. After a jury trial and direct appeal, I was given a thirty-five-year prison sentence. Fast forward nineteen years to the present and here I sit, living in the full grace of God and walking the path he has afforded me by earning a Christian liberal arts education. I am fully convinced that, while God is not confined to any human presupposition when it comes to transforming lives, he is the Redeemer that can properly utilize the roles of educator and student, to transform any life no matter what stage it is in or path it is on. Noted educator, author, and theologian C. S. Lewis wrote in his essay "Learning in War-Time" that "The intellectual life is not the only road to God . . . but we find it to be a road, and it may be the appointed road for us."[1] Despite my extremely rough start and my long and winding path of on-again, off-again educational opportunities, God has further fully enriched my life through every step of it. I earned an associate degree in behavioral science from Western Oklahoma State College in May 2019, and I am currently beginning my senior year of a bachelor's degree program in Christian studies from Oklahoma Baptist University, made possible through the Prison Divinity Program. In both of those college settings, I was, in my mind, changed for the better and I was able to experience growth in my worldview.

So, I ardently assert that true life transformation is possible for anyone through the redemption, regeneration, and restoration that can be found in belief and discipleship in Jesus Christ. I just as ardently claim that it is in the discipling of others—when willing teachers and willing students meet under the guidance of the Holy Spirit—that true life transformation is able to take place. My point being that a redeeming rehabilitative environment consisting of Christian-based counseling and the pursuit of education will be an environment that self-propagates qualities of healing and wholeness. Just as Jesus Christ represents the opportunity for broken humanity to be made whole and to be redeemed for God's purposes, a Christocentric liberal arts education and its resulting Christocentric worldview represents an opportunity to reinvest the love we have been given—to replant, if you will, those seeds of faith that were first sown in us in whatever community we found ourselves in. Thus stated, our purpose is to change the paradigm of our life culture by bringing healing and wholeness to broken human lives and, yes, to a broken system of justice and corrections that says rehabilitation and education have no place in prison. Our

1. Lewis, "Learning in War-Time," 50.

calling is to do this by educating ourselves and others through the good news that teaches that true redemption, reconciliation, healing, and purpose is possible for everyone in Jesus Christ, no matter where they are.

As I conclude by reflecting back on the pieces of my story I have shared with you, I see potential that was not met at that time due to a lack of parental and personal cultivation as well as the failings of a public school system of overworked educators and administrators striving to maintain said system. I make no assignations as to place blame, as any and all reasons for a school system being in dire straits stems from a combination of factors. Nevertheless, the school system I was part of had not quite evolved and perhaps was primarily geared toward moving as many people through its system as possible with little regard for how students made it through, if they made it through, or what happened to them after they did or did not make it. Aristotle might refer to this as education with no heart. It should be easy to see that any individual with a lack in their parental and personal cultivation soon finds themselves reliant upon some other mainstay in their life for said cultivation of their young life. While the school system and its educators may not have asked for this responsibility, they have nevertheless been burdened and tasked with this responsibility. This is because for some students school becomes a place where they feel safe enough to trust the adults around them and seek familial support. This may be a burden, but I say it is better that the school system be the closest approximation a student might have to a family than some gang. I found myself in the latter situation back then, and it was within such an overburdened system, lacking in the ability to pay attention to some students and meet their needs, where I fell through the cracks and into oblivion.

My story may have relevance for application in a few ways. First, for educators of every stripe: you are recognized and you are loved, so please do not grow weary in doing good. Many of you chose your profession out of a heart to serve and not for the money. Whether that still holds true or not, I understand that you want your efforts to be a cause for the world to become a better place through the lives you have influence over. I also know that, sometimes, some of those young lives lose their way no matter what you do; even so, please keep doing everything you can to find the strength, wisdom, and love to continue reaching out to those entrusted to your teaching and care. Believe this: what you do every day out of self-sacrificing love (also referred to as αγαπε or *agape love*) does matter and it does have significant influence because, as the Reverend Dr. Martin Luther King Jr. proclaimed, "through love, potentiality becomes actuality."[2] So, whether the agape love you expend daily in the teaching of your students manifests fruit now or sometime later, it *will* manifest because agape love cannot help but bring forth actuality out of potentiality.

Second, for students: be strong, be courageous, and be patient with yourselves and those around you as you grow in wisdom and agape love. Namely, because there is a purpose in everything you are being asked to learn, just as there is a purpose in seeking to understand anything for yourself. The purpose of learning from those who have come before you is to incorporate firsthand knowledge that redeems you from having to experience what may be uncomfortable, if not outright dangerous, to yourself. This is for your benefit and not to dissuade you from having questions about life or to dissuade you from experiencing life for yourself. No, this is simply so you can make informed choices about critical life decisions for yourself based on the previous real-time evidence of others. Because the truth is that some decisions have generational effects. I promise you that a heart and mind that is open to instruction, knowledge, and understanding as a youth is a heart and mind that never stops yearning to pass on that legacy of knowledge and understanding to others as an adult. You only serve to limit yourself and whatever potential it is you do have by not listening and learning from those who have come before you. It is an even greater fallacy to believe that any human from whatever ancient epoch has little or nothing to offer to us here in our modern epoch with our modern technologies. C. S. Lewis referred

---

2. King Jr., *Strength to Love*, 50.

to this as "chronological snobbery."[3] Do not be a chrono-snob in your youth and the adult you will thank you later for your wisdom.

Third, for the imprisoned: look at me, there is a love that was sacrificed to give all of the world hope and this agape love will come and reconcile, heal, teach, and restore anyone who asks him to. His name is Jesus of Nazareth and he proclaimed that "The Spirit of the Lord God is on Me, because the Lord has anointed Me to bring good news to the poor. He has sent Me to heal the brokenhearted, to proclaim liberty to the captives and freedom to the prisoners; to proclaim the year of the Lord's favor."[4] I should not have to spell this out for anyone, but this is literally good news. Do any of you have broken hearts? Do any of you want to be set free from some things? Do any of you wish to have real liberty? Do any of you desire to be made well? Jesus Christ has made the way for everyone to have all of those things. You are not confined to being forever known as whatever broken thing it is your family, friends, society, and your judgment and sentence says you are. Jesus can break every generational curse and allow you to stop living whatever dehumanizing lie has been laid upon you. Allow yourself to be forgiven and healed of every burden you have laid upon yourself. Repent, believe, and allow yourself to be loved by the One who created you, redeems you, sustains you, and who will transform you. Jesus says to arise, pick up your mat, and follow him because the One calling you is merciful and faithful.

JAMES JOSEPH WYMER JR.

James Joseph "Buster" Wymer Jr. is a lover of God, family, reading, writing, and music. He was born in Lawton, Oklahoma, to sixteen-year-old parents. He was raised on the southeast side of Oklahoma City by family until his arrest on December 15, 1992. He received a ten-year, four-month incarceration in the Oklahoma City Jail and the Oklahoma Department of Corrections between

---

3. Lewis, *Surprised by Joy*, 207–8.
4. Luke 4:16–21; cf. Isa 61:1–2.

the ages of sixteen and twenty-six. Upon his release in 2003, he worked hard to get into the flow of family and community life. Unfortunately, after only a year of freedom and struggling to deal with a lifelong meth addiction, he found himself participating in a meth transaction-turned-burglary, for which he was arrested. A year after that, James was on his way back to prison with a thirty-five-year sentence. In the ensuing nineteen years of incarceration, God has used this time to redeem James by giving him the opportunity to attend college. With this opportunity, James has earned an associate degree in behavioral science in 2019 and he is currently working on earning a bachelor's degree in Christian studies from Oklahoma Baptist University.

BIBLIOGRAPHY

Christian Standard Bible. Nashville: Holman Bible, 2018.
King, Martin Luther, Jr. *Strength to Love*. Minneapolis: Fortress, 2010.
Lewis, C. S. "Learning in War-Time." In *The Weight of Glory and Other Addresses*, 43–54. New York: Macmillan, 1949.
———. *Surprised by Joy*. New York: HarperOne, 2017.

You Can, You Will

Christopher Evans

I NEVER IMAGINED I would attend a university, never mind doing so twice. Yet here I am in prison and attending Oklahoma Baptist University's Prison Divinity Program. Previously, I attended Rose State College (RSC) in Midwest City, Oklahoma, and squandered the opportunity of an induction into Phi Theta Kappa, a prestigious group for high academic achievers. The opportunity of an education is a blessing. Before arriving at the Lexington Assessment and Reception Center for a second time, I developed the misconception that, as a twenty-four-year-old man, I knew how to learn. I allowed myself to think that my life experiences and sharp intellect meant I should know how to do anything required in any educational setting. I was wrong. What follows is my experience with failure while learning how to learn.

I SHOULD KNOW HOW

The hard truth is that I did not know how to write an MLA-style paper. Before attending RSC, I could not format on Microsoft Word. While attending OBU, I had to learn how to use Turabian format and *The Chicago Manual of Style*. I then had to learn how to adjust the settings in the Microsoft Word program. Although my previous education experience taught me how to use MLA and APA formats, Turabian format was foreign and confusing. My ego led me to try to figure out these things on my own. The first paper Dr. Bruce Perkins, professor and the PDP director, graded was, in my opinion, a disastrous failure. I did not have the expertise necessary to write the paper nor did I seek help. I learned that I must learn by asking for help.

The Prison Divinity Program began with a brief semester in the summer of 2021. I began the semester thinking it would be an easy A. The courses were not loaded with due dates or hundreds of pages of reading. Still, I struggled to have the assigned reading done on time. I felt intense pressure to meet the required due dates. The class schedule still conflicts with the everyday prison functions (e.g., lunch, count time, unit staff office hours, medical appointments, and property room hours), which adds to the frustration. The pre-semester was the most difficult because no one knew what to expect from the warden or the Oklahoma Department of Corrections city office. Many times, inmates across the facility are placed on longer than normal lockdowns, which interferes with class times and due dates. Our schedules are constantly changing. The one certainty is uncertainty. For this reason, the greatest lesson I embrace is that of adhering to a schedule.

I remember attending a lecture on scheduling and study methods. This lecture was an immense help. I learned to write out my assignments and due dates on a calendar and color code each class. Additionally, I decided to color code due dates according to the assignment percentages in the class. For example, when I have a major assignment worth 20 percent or more of the grade in a specific class I highlight them in a bright color, which signifies importance and urgency. If I am using a paper calendar, I write all tests in red. If the calendar is in digital format, I will type the tests with red letters and highlight assignments in a bright color. A benefit of this method is the assignments are easily recognizable from the tests. Another benefit is that the days between assignments can become study or research days.

A week in advance of all tests, I will schedule time to study. For example, I will schedule one or two hours each day for review, if time permits, leading up to the test day. For major assignments, I schedule research time every other day. I use the every-other-day method so that I am able to prepare for the next class lecture.

When I write assignments, I use a little different method. I usually write while researching to ensure adequate representation of the information found during the research process. I never research more than two hours at a time. When I exceed the two-hour limit, I find myself spending more time falling down rabbit holes rather than remaining focused on the topic at hand. This experience taught me to stay on the initial scheduled times from the beginning of the semester. I continue to have more than enough time to read, research, write, and study in the event of a schedule change that results in pushing off due dates or lectures. Sticking to the first schedule allows me to achieve high marks.

LEARNING IS A POSITIVE HABIT

Learning while incarcerated continues to offer new challenges. During this journey, I have dealt with being locked in a small, cramped cell and have experienced violent interruptions, the prejudices of the ODOC, and the negativity of inmates seeking to destroy my ambition. Very quickly, I had to set it in my mind that I would not fail! Therefore, I continue to remind myself of my abilities and capabilities. Every morning, I wake up and repeat these words: "I can learn, I am learning, and I am a worthy investment." Our current societies do not understand the value of the inmate population. I cannot recall the number of times I heard the ODOC staff, who come into prison from free company, say things like "those pieces of $#?! don't deserve a free education," to try to demoralize the inmates within earshot. When people hear negative opinions like that, they latch onto them and repeat them. The next thing you know, that negativity spreads with an intense following. For this reason, OBU is special. We are taught to rely upon God, to think deep and wide about society and the competing ideologies within it. We learn to find solutions, create plans, and build systems of change with God at the tip of the spear of change.

Negative pressures of any kind can creep into your mind, especially when they are frequent and widespread. Therefore, you have to combat them just as frequently with positive affirmations that you believe are true. Developing a positive mindset is one way to begin embracing an education that you may feel is above your worth. *You can do more.* Western civilization courses and doctrine courses taught me to focus on the power of God, which enables me to do more.

Continual reflection on personal worth keeps me focused on my value. That is great! I can recall a time when I thought so highly of myself that my education lost its value. I was walking from my cell to the classroom and the thought of dropping out and educating myself shot into the forefront of my mind. I had never tried self-education before, yet here I was thinking I could do better than the men and women who have dedicated themselves to the dissemination of highly intellectual information to unlearned people with different capabilities of learning. Looking back now, I laugh at my naïveté. I have learned that I am never worth more than I am when I join God in his work wherever I am, including in my education. Think about this: education is so important to God that he had men write down his words and history in numerous languages so all of the world can learn about him.

I now understand the education I am receiving is a direct result of hundreds of years of study and distillation from many scholars. Over those years, scholars have devoted their entire lives to study in order to ensure its accuracy. I have come to realize that the information is not just some stuff in books but is the history of society. Our history benefits those who hope to avoid making serious mistakes that could cost lives. Therefore, I find it most beneficial to learn from the most dedicated.

I find great relief in knowing that someone else walked this path before me. The pressure is off of me to focus on novel discoveries. Although new ideas come, I focus on learning what is established and I let the rest come as it may. After all, students are students of what is known. The progression of education eventually leads to new discoveries. Therefore, there is no reason to spend an intense amount of time on seeking the undiscovered before knowing what is known.

What I am trying to say is take your time learning what is in front of you.

FAILURE IS NOT AN F

I have not received an F on an assignment, test, or course in a long time, although I *can* remember the last one. The last F I received was in high school. It was my junior year at Del City High School and my efforts were less than acceptable. I skipped school, ignored due dates, never prepared for any of my classes, and used drugs. I had cooked up a recipe for disaster. I learned that I failed myself instead of an assignment. I learned I did not have to continue to fail, as long as I applied myself in the right way. That idea is 99 percent of the battle.

It must be understood that even if you work hard and study hard, you may still fail. That is just part of life. Failure is just another building block of achievement. The best part of missing the mark is learning to hit the mark. With every new attempt, you gain knowledge. That knowledge will get you closer and closer to high achievements. Here is the secret: you must be willing to learn from your mistakes and apply what you learned. Without application of the lessons inherent in every mistake, you will continue to fail in the same way you failed before.

You may be reading this and rolling your eyes. You may be thinking, "What a cliché." If you are, then I want you to know something: I had to learn from my mistakes in life. I continue to apply what I learned in my academic endeavors. I have yet to miss an opportunity to make the President's Honor Roll. Attending OBU is different from other schools because the professors care about the success of their students and go the extra mile to ensure that their students can obtain achievements like the President's Honor Roll.

When I thought about all the "could haves" and "would haves," I knew I had to do something different. I could not continue to skate through different situations in life and expect to be successful. Losing the opportunity at RSC, losing my first business, and coming back to prison were big revelations. The biggest was realizing I will not be able to watch my son grow up. I will not be a part of his transformative moments in life. Therefore, when the opportunity to be a part of the PDP came along I knew it was the last chance I would have to prove to myself, my family, and to society that I am better than what I have been. If I squandered the opportunity of reflection and application, I would still be failing. I would be a failure to my family, to society, and to myself.

Maybe you have not gone through similar situations in your life. Maybe you do not think you will have to learn such difficult lessons. That is amazing and I am truly happy for you. Maybe you are that person, but you are struggling in school because you just do not know what to do. I hope you will take a lesson from what I am sharing in this short chapter and apply it in your own life. I hope your biggest takeaway from this section is that *you are only a failure if you refuse to learn from your mistakes and apply what you learn.*

FACILITY STAFF

Another issue I continue to navigate is learning to adjust to new professors. I understand professors have a very busy schedule and teach many students. Often times, professors teach multiple courses with varying degrees of depth. I believe it is the student's responsibility to adjust to the professor's style of teaching.

As a student, I begin each class by asking questions that relate to learning. What kind of tests does the professor normally administer for the course? What does the professor require when writing papers? Does the professor prefer one writing style or is the professor flexible? Will the professor make his/her lectures available for review and study?

The first test is the best gauge for determining how to study. If the professor asks you to explain a topic, then you would give in-depth information proving you have an overall understanding of the topic. If the professor asks you to discuss a topic, then you would give the main points of the topic and then give in-depth information.

HELPFUL REMINDERS

Facility staff have a lot on their plate. As a student, it is helpful to remember that students are not the only priority of the staff. If you are having problems studying, I suggest finding a study group or starting a study group.

Students have a lot of stress and responsibility. It is helpful if staff remembers that a student attends school hoping to change their lives for the better. Usually, a couple of failures will take a student down the path of lethargic performance. Those students need encouragement and support. Students have real-life situations (deaths, marriages, children, jobs, etc.) that can prompt a downturn and affect their performance, attendance, and attitudes. I think crisis intervention training for staff would greatly improve students' chances of success.

SUMMARY

As a student, you are in college to learn. You will make mistakes and that is exactly how you will learn. Learning is not always about making the best grade. Yes, awesome grades will open doors and get awards, yet awesome grades will *not* help you learn, retain, and apply what you have learned. The best way to succeed is to learn to apply. Learning to apply will always bring a positive outcome and ensure positive habits. Applying what you learn will prove you can succeed.

Staff members have a tough job and a busy schedule. Professors, assistants, security staff, wardens, and administrators have tough jobs! Yet there is never a substitute for a staff member willing to help a student succeed. Properly trained staff members are those who are able to identify the struggling student and encourage their efforts.

Staff and student must work together. I have heard it said, "It takes a village to raise a man." A campus and an institution is exactly that—a village. Their inhabitants, whether student, staff, or inmate are the villagers trying to raise an adult. Working together is the only way to ensure all succeed. Working together means we will succeed.

CHRISTOPHER EVANS

During middle school and high school, Christopher Evans was fortunate enough to walk away with A's and B's. His mother held academics in high regard and would not let him fail. Before he could finish school, he went to prison and obtained his GED with scores in the top five-to-ten percentile in Oklahoma. He attended Rose State College but children and other circumstances thwarted his goal of graduation. As a result of hard work and planning, he is now close to graduating from Oklahoma Baptist University with honors.

Encouraging Non-Catholics and Non-Protestants in Christian Colleges

Edsel Hill

MY FAMILY CONSISTS OF Baptists, Catholics, and Mormons. I have been baptized in all three churches. I am now a member of the Living Church of God (LCG), which does not believe in a Trinity, does not keep Christmas or Easter, but does keep the commandments and original holy days, which include Saturday Sabbaths and the seven High Holy Sabbath Feast Days (Pentecost, Tabernacles, etc.). With over 180 college hours from Cameron University and Western Oklahoma State College, I have not completed a bachelor's degree. I do have an associate degree in behavioral science. Getting a bachelor's degree is a lifelong goal. I was not sure what to expect from the PDP, since I knew that I held different beliefs than the Baptists. My wife is Baptist and we get along, so I expected to get along with others here. It did not go as I expected, since others disagreed with my beliefs. I would like this opportunity to talk about some of the problems that I encountered and solutions that were discovered. God and prayer have helped me to endeavor to persevere. If possible, I would like to help others who hold different beliefs traverse the difficulties that may arise in the PDP and OBU classes.

OVERCOMING RIDICULE AND HARMFUL COMMENTS AS AN OUTSIDER

To begin, I will share my personal reflections that showcase the most important aspects of my educational journey. In the OBU classroom, ridiculing has progressed to include the salient, religious aspect of my identity. By salient, I mean this aspect is important and that my religion often receives the attention and ridicule of others. I am a Christian seeking biblical truths, but I am not a Protestant or Catholic like most of the students and professors. I am a member of the LCG, which worships the Father and Son—called *Elohim*, meaning the God Family—as mentioned in the Bible. We keep the commandments, not falsely believing that they are done away. We keep God's Saturday Sabbaths, not Sundays. We keep God's Holy Days, not the pagan-originated holidays of Christmas, Easter, New Year's, and birthdays. Nowhere in the Bible is the Holy Spirit worshipped, called God, or shown to communicate with the Father and Son. Since the pagan Trinity has been around for over five thousand years, we do not adopt it in place of the God Family of the Bible. The Bible and our beliefs do not include a Trinity with the Holy Spirit being God. If you are a Catholic or Protestant, chances are that you disagreed with and got angry at this whole paragraph. Now you might understand why students, staff, chaplains, and professors have ridiculed me about my religion. I can prove my beliefs through the Bible, which are different from their beliefs and traditions.

The flyer for OBU attendance said that the program is "open to people with any religion or no religion at all." I am writing to share with those of any or no religion. I want to help those who may be like me and believe differently from mainstream Catholics and Protestants. I want to say up front that the educational knowledge has been invaluable in helping me to draw closer to and to know God better. I love studying the Bible and learning new things about

ENCOURAGING NON-CATHOLICS AND NON-PROTESTANTS

God. The problems happen when I talk about my beliefs. If you sit in class and keep your beliefs to yourself, you will not encounter the responses that I have gotten. If you do speak up, you may encounter different or similar responses. Here are some comments that I received from students, staff, chaplains, and professors.

> "Why are you even in this program if you don't believe like we do and aren't even Baptist?" "All twelve things you just said about your beliefs were totally wrong and disagree with what we believe." "Since the commandments are done away, we don't have to obey the 'do not lie' command. We are under the New Testament that says to obey those in authority. So, when staff tells you to lie on paperwork, you are to obey God by obeying authority figures." "Edsel never closes his eyes to pray with us." "Have you considered that we don't have a different God, but just a different perspective of the same God?" to which I replied, "The Father and Son are the biblical God Family consisting of two separate Beings, which is totally different from the similar God perspectives of Buddhists, Pagans, Trinitarians, Muslims, Taoists, etc." "I have heard of God only being one person, the Father, and of God as the Trinity, but I have never heard of God being two separate persons of Father and Son." "Don't listen to anything Edsel says. He's deceived by Satan so every word out of his mouth is a lie." "You are welcome to any chapel class that we teach, but you follow the father of lies. We will not listen to you teach lies at Purpose Driven Life or at any class you teach. We told the Christians not to go either. You need to find non-Christians for your class." I had two people attend the class. When I was asked to attend some of my fellow students' chapel classes, I said, "I will support you the way you support me. You reap what you sow." The response was, "We are doing God's work and you need to start doing it with us and quit serving the devil." I spend four to six hours a day in Bible study. I get responses such as: "There you are again writing the Bible according to Edsel," "If you don't like what it says, just change it like Edsel does," and "I guess what God said isn't good enough. Are you still fixing his mistakes?"

PART III. STORIES OF PERSONAL PERSPECTIVES

I was asked, "Can you just shut up and quit asking questions in class? You are the reason classes go late. Your questions are all jokes and make fun of what we believe. You are never serious about God and the truth."

I intentionally grouped all the comments from different persons together so no one person could be identified by others. This paper was not written to be an attack or retaliation against anyone. Most controversies have come from classmates.

CONTINUING TO ENDURE, APOLOGIZE, AND PERSIST AS A LEARNER

Next, my reflections are applied concerning the most salient aspects of my educational journey through a significant life experience that led to transformative teaching and learning. I am in prison for a murder committed in 1999. When I came to prison, gangsters influenced my behavior to become angry and violent. I was seconds away from killing a person in prison in 2008. After that experience, I promised God I would never hurt another person ever again if he would help me know his truths in the Bible. As I said earlier, my family members are Baptists, Catholics, and Mormons, and I have been baptized into all three of these churches. They did not help me stay out of prison, and they all taught different doctrines. As I sought truth from God in the Bible, I learned two important messages about life from the LCG. I learned the meaning of Elohim and that I can be part of that family someday. I also learned the commandments are not done away, including the Sabbaths and the Holy Days. I learned to be responsible for my actions, sins, and thoughts. I sought to be a peacemaker, as I had promised God I would be in 2008.

I spent the next fourteen years learning to control myself. I still got angry, but I did not stoop to physical violence. This affected my life and development in unforeseen ways. By my seeking the real God, he revealed himself and his Church to me. The more that I kept the commandments, Sabbaths, and Holy Days, the easier it became to be a peacemaker and resist violence. Then

I came to OBU, and my beliefs came under attack. Other students spoke against my beliefs until I became violent again. I had not lost my temper in fourteen years in some of the toughest, gang-filled prisons in Oklahoma. Instead, some ridiculing by Christian students pulled me out of my walk with God. I had made a promise of nonviolence to God on that day in 2008 when I almost killed a man. The day I broke that promise changed my life. I would have dropped out of OBU if Dr. Perkins had not talked me into staying in class. He said a lot, but what I recollect most is that we all backslide and sin, but God continuously forgives when we repent. He asked if I believed God brought me into the program. Did I believe God was done teaching me, or did he have more that I needed to learn? I spoke at the chapel about breaking my promise to be a peacemaker in front of OBU students. I apologized, thanked Dr. Perkins for his help, and recommitted myself to serving God as a nonviolent peacemaker. The lasting impact of this experience is that I avoid any extracurricular activities with OBU students that may lead to religious controversies. I spend time praying daily to God and studying. Since I spoke publicly at the chapel, things have gotten better in the classroom. Communication and prayers have helped eliminate past problems. I help when someone seeks my assistance in class studies, but I ask hardly any religious questions in class. I ask them on my own time, usually by emails to the professors.

STRATEGIES FOR CREATING GREATER FORTITUDE AND MORE INCLUSIVE LEARNING ENVIRONMENTS

Finally, I will share my insights on how best to embrace learning based on your own experience. I hinted at some strategies and suggestions above, such as daily prayer, communication, apologizing, and talking to Christian authority figures such as Dr. Perkins for advice. I also email my minister often, and discuss issues with him when he visits. I can also call various LCG members. Whatever your beliefs, it is important to stay in contact with your church for support. Another suggestion is to stay busy by helping others; this will keep your mind on God and your neighbors, not yourself. Along with what I mentioned above, remember that truly listening to others provides ideas for improving their lives. Improvements can be made through physical assistance like changing a tire or a diaper; emotional assistance, such as listening to someone while they vent their educational or family problems or feelings; or even spiritual assistance, which can be accomplished by improving their Christian walks with God and teaching the gospel of the kingdom. Most people would prefer to live a good life with family as opposed to a bad one in prison. They may think physical things should be present in a good life, such as food, water, clothing, and a safe, clean place to live. Emotional things should be present in a good life, such as friends, family, and authority figures in areas like education, safety, and health. Spiritual things should be present in a good life, such as access to Bibles and other religious materials, your church family, religious freedom, and authority figures such as ministers and deacons.

The family, friends, and authority figures mentioned above can help those in different situations. I grew up alone as an outcast and was mostly self-educated through reading for hours in school libraries. I have learned the value of education and the curse of being an outcast. Now I try to help anyone needing educational assistance. I help those feeling dejected grow to feel like a part of society. I want others to have what I do not have even today, to feel like they are a normal part of something. I am slowly becoming part of the OBU community, but classes end in a year and a half. Even the chaplain wrote on my evaluation that I was a loner and that I was not part of the Catholic or Protestant communities. He said I still do not fit in and could leave the program today if I wanted. My strengths as a helper are that I truly care about others and have the time as well as the physical and spiritual resources to help them. My weaknesses in helping are that I have terrible social skills, such as difficulty remembering names. The many group assignments and discussions have forced me to associate with other students. There is no hiding in the library anymore. Helping others and spreading the gospel has helped my communication skills.

Some people's biases and prejudices concerning my lazy eye might have interfered with my ability to mature and become an effective helper sooner in life. Their comments may include my being clumsy, handicapped, abnormal looking, socially awkward, nerdy, or even slights of my religious beliefs. I have developed some biases of my own while in prison. I have mentioned that my family believes in different religions. I was baptized into those religions and had nothing against them until I came to prison and experienced religious controversies. My family consists of whites, blacks, Mexicans, and Indians. I had no racial prejudices until I came to prison. I now avoid gangs of every race. In other words, I used to avoid everyone equally. It was just safer and more peaceful being on my own. Previously, I would have helped anyone who asked for it. It is different now. I now ask if they need help and bring the gospel slowly into conversations. I will pray for my Christian enemies, but I find it difficult being around them at times. I do my best to avoid situations of potential ridicule for my beliefs. I feel most drawn to work with those who have been rejected as I have been rejected, such as other loners and outcasts of different beliefs. I have compassion for their pain and want to help them before they go through all I have experienced. God is using the program to teach me how to mature my social skills and associate with others.

CONCLUSION

This essay encouraged thoughtful self-reflection and self-examination. Its purpose was to write about how my program experiences could help others. As I tried to reason things out, I began to understand God's purpose for bringing me here. In this essay, I wrote some brief details, including information on who I was before, who I am becoming now, an overview of my life experiences and influences, as well as the benefits of learning helping skills. By doing this, I learned something about myself. Promising God that I would not sin by physical violence does not prevent me from physically harming others. I can be violent even if I desire to be a peacemaker. I can be prejudiced even if I do not want to be. I can have animosity to Christians, be mean to them, and call them names. I need to forgive others as I need God to forgive me. I need God's help to overcome because on my own I am just a sinner. This program has been illuminating.

EDSEL HILL

Edsel Hill was born with a lazy eye handicap. Because he was not normal-looking, he was targeted and picked on from kindergarten onward. He was never invited to any events like birthday parties or sleepovers. He never developed social skills and spent many hours in libraries, reading thousands of books. Through these experiences, he learned to fight and defend himself. He had over 180 college credit hours before coming to prison. He learned to make jokes and enjoy life with his wife and five children. God called to him and changed him by bringing him to into this program.

Epilogue

Antonio Chiareli

THIS PAST SPRING SEMESTER (2024), I once again had the privilege to offer my Introduction to Sociology course for OBU's Prison Divinity Program. This time around, most of my questions, worries, and anxieties about teaching at the Lexington Correctional Facility were already dealt with by the start of the semester, since I had offered this same course two years prior and my experience then was overwhelmingly positive. So, I genuinely looked forward to another great semester with "the guys."

Looking back over this past spring semester, I have come away with deep gratitude to our Lord Jesus Christ for the opportunity to teach yet another outstanding group of students, who certainly did not disappoint. There are many things for which I am thankful, and I would like to briefly convey here some of the most significant reasons why this program and these students are a gift of light in a world that cries out for redemption.

I am again amazed at how God continues to transform these men's lives through this program. I don't know what kind of students they were in their past lives, but I can assert that the light of Christ was evident in their conduct and seriousness about my course during every single class session. In fact, I would say that this group proved to me yet again that teaching sociology to students in this program is one of the most rewarding and satisfying experiences a sociology professor can hope for. This is because they see sociology through a different prism than most traditional students at OBU's Shawnee campus. Through their learning process, they were able to make concrete connections between their lived experience and sociological theory and concepts. Sociology, especially when well-integrated with a Christian faith perspective, speaks directly to their notions about the social world, empirical reality, and their place in society, and it is exciting to see these students grasp and begin to exercise the "Sociological Imagination," or the ability to establish links between our lives and society as a whole. Because of what they've already been through in life and, importantly, because of what they have also learned in other PDP courses, these students were able to develop amazing insights and they grew in their perspicacity for critical thinking. These are reasons to give God praise for his transformative work in these students' lives, and for showing us how an authentically Christian liberal arts education can re-enchant students, beckoning them to a new God-centered vision of themselves, their place in the world, and their role in God's kingdom.

I cannot end here without mentioning one more excellent and praiseworthy impression this program and these students have left me with. As I watched them grow more knowledgeable and bolder in their understanding of Christ's preeminence in all things, it became evident to me that this program's equipping of these students has also raised their consciousness about how they want to use this wisdom. As the semester progressed, they seemed more empowered to articulate their views and even their ideas for solutions to issues they face as incarcerated men. They demonstrated surprisingly nuanced and sophisticated perspectives about their lives behind bars, and I believe that they can serve as a voice of reasonableness and wisdom about their experience as inmates to those of us on the outside. What I mean is, perhaps there may be a way that OBU can serve as a conduit to facilitate communication and advocate for principled, just, and humane solutions to the issues that affect those in prison in our state. Great Christian minds are being cultivated in the PDP. One of the ways we can obey Christ's exhortation to "visit those in prison" may be to allow them a voice to make a restorative contribution to society even while behind bars.

I praise God for what he has indeed been doing in OBU's Prison Divinity Program, and I pray it will continue to succeed and bear much good fruit for the glory of the Name.

In Christ,
Toni

www.ingramcontent.com/pod-product-compliance
Lightning Source LLC
Chambersburg PA
CBHW022113160426
43197CB00009B/1006